COMPUTER TECHNOLOGY AND EMPLOYMENT

This is a book on the present, with reference to the past, and a glimpse to the future. The reality of the future, in terms of work and work processes, the participation of people in work activity, the organisation of enterprises and institutions, and interpersonal and personal–institutional relationships, is radically different from the reality of the present. An issue of critical importance is the extent to which the people as workers and participants in economic and social activity will accommodate the new reality.

The historical reality is a source of comfort: the reality of the present is radically different from the reality of the past; yet, accommodations to change have been successful, and generally beneficial to the large majority of the population. The significant issue is not the nature of the change, but rather the rate of change, and the time period over which the change takes place. In the very distant future utopia is reality, just as the present is utopia to the distant past.

The phase of microelectronic technology in effect over the past 25 years is only the first of a three-phase evolutionary process. It is characterised by largely stand-alone instruments and processes, such as computers, word processors, and copiers, each designed to perform some specific ranges of work functions. Their effect on work activity has been to expand it beyond what was done or could have been done by the instruments and processes that existed prior to the introduction of microelectronics. As a result, their impact on employment has been generally positive. New occupations and new employments have been created, and the increase in output of goods and services associated directly with the employment of microelectronic instruments and processes created further employment throughout the economy.

But, while the employment effect of the first phase may have been positive, the employment effects of the second and third phases are less certain, and will require careful monitoring and appropriate corrective measures.

The second phase will come into being when the stand-alone instruments and processes become linked together into systems of communication and work processing within enterprises and institutions. The initial steps of implementation of this phase have been taken, and by the end of the decade it should be commonplace. But its effect on employment will likely be minimal, since external communication will remain as heretofore – by post, messenger, and telephone. As long as the convergence of computers and telecommunications technologies into telematic systems remains limited to activities that are internal to enterprises, duplicate communications systems will have to be maintained – one for internal communication and another, a conventional one, for external communication. The effect on employment will likely remain positive.

The third phase is the critical phase for employment. This is the phase when the telematic systems of individual enterprises and institutions become linked together into a telematic network of the nature of the telephone network. When this becomes reality, profound effects on employment and society at large will be recorded. The reality of this phase is utopia to the present. Description of the processes of work, the nature of human participation in work, communication amongst people and between people, enterprises and institutions assumes science fiction elements. No purpose can be served by naratives on human participation in processes of production and on employment in economic and social environments that border on science fiction.

Stephen G. Peitchinis is Professor of Economics at the University of Calgary, Canada, and a consultant to government and industry on matters related to technology and employment.

His previous publications include *The Economics of Labour, Labour–Management Relations in the Railway Industry, The Canadian Labour Market* and *The Implication of Technological Changes for the Educational and Skill Requirements of Industry*.

COMPUTER TECHNOLOGY AND EMPLOYMENT

Retrospect and Prospect

STEPHEN G. PEITCHINIS

MACMILLAN PRESS
LONDON

First published 1983 by
THE MACMILLAN PRESS LTD
London and Basingstoke
Companies and representatives throughout the world

ISBN 0 333 35330 7

Printed in Hong Kong

To Jacquelyn

Contents

List of Tables

Acknowledgements

I started the research for this book in 1976, when I was commissioned by the Technology Branch of the Department of Industry, Trade and Commerce of Canada to investigate 'the effects of technological changes on the educational and skill requirements of industry'. The investigation resulted in a series of studies on the general issue of the relationship between technology and employment, including a study of 'the employment implications of computers and telecommunications technology' for the Department of Communications of Canada. I am indebted to a number of people in those two departments for their support and advice, particularly to Tom Clarke, Jack Scrimgeour, Jennifer Rose and Shirley Serafini.

I prepared the manuscript during my appointment to a Killam Resident Research Fellowship at The University of Calgary, in Alberta, Canada. I am pleased to acknowledge my gratitude to the University of Calgary and the Killam Foundation.

I have discussed many of the ideas presented in the book with scores of people, and benefited significantly from the discussions. I would be remiss if I did not name specifically Tom Clarke, formerly of the Department of Industry, Trade and Commerce of Canada, and Dr Zavis Zeman, Director of the Technology and Society Programme, of the Institute for Research on Public Policy.

Amongst the most onerous work functions associated with the research and writing of a book must be the secretarial and typing. I acknowledge the efficiency and competence of Elma Kaufman and Maureen Samuels.

STEPHEN G. PEITCHINIS

Acknowledgements

1 Reality and Fiction

Introduction

This is a book on the present, with reference to the past, and a glimpse to the future. The past we know only as well as history has recorded it; the present is transitional, and as such experiences continuous changes; and the future is uncertain.

The reality of the future, in terms of work processes, human participation in work activity, the organisation of enterprises and institutions, and social interactions generally, is radically different from the present. But, then, the reality of the present is radically different from the reality of the past. The question is how distant is the past with which we compare, and how distant the future to which we make reference. In the very distant future utopia is reality, just as the present is utopia to the distant past.

The Effects of 'Technology'

The effects of technology are a much discussed topic. To some, technology is an opportunity; to others it is a source of uncertainty and concern. Some regard it absolutely essential for our survival, others view it with trepidation. The electronics engineer, the systems analyst, the software specialist, and those who look at the economy in its general state – on the aggregate – will be in the first group; printers, telephone operators, railway workers, elevator constructors, and assembly line workers will be in the second group.

Both groups can point to some reality in support of their individual positions. The question is to what extent can we extrapolate and generalise from the experiences of individual groups. The historical experience teaches us to avoid reaching general conclusions on the basis of limited premises, and the fallacy of composition tells us that in many instances what is true in individual cases is not necessarily true in the general context. One person can become rich by saving most of his income; if all the people were to save most of their incomes, unemployment will increase, incomes will fall, savings will be exhausted, and all will become poor.

There is a general tendency to identify and emphasise aspects of technological changes that have had or are associated with negative effects on society. We all know that science and technology are primarily responsible for the tremendous increase in living standards over the past century. Yet, when we talk of the industrial revolution and employment, people do not usually think of the employment that was created, rather of the employment that was destroyed. People think of the Luddite riots (1811–19) when workers smashed the machines;[1] they think of the atom bomb and its tremendous destructive potential; and they think of how technology has changed society and destroyed the 'good old days'. But, even those who miss the good old days would, on reflection, admit that the reality of the good old days was not so good for the vast majority of the people. A positive and fortunate characteristic of human life is the common tendency not to feel experiences of sorrow, hardship and deprivation with the passage of time. Because of this, the reality of the past assumes fictional dimensions. Strip any reality of the good and you have a fictional nightmare; strip any reality of the bad and you have a fictional bliss.

The reality or fiction of *the past* is a matter of interpretation. But, the application of such one-sided assessment to *the present* can create serious problems with scientific and technological development. The bad side highlights unemployment, pollution, disruption of long-established social values, and the Frankenstein consequences of genetic experimentation. The good side emphasises the increase in productivity and incomes, the significant improvements in transportation and communication, the eradication of some serious diseases, and the implicit promises of scientific and technological experimentation for improvements in living standards and general social welfare.

Each side emphasises a fictional scenario. Reality contains elements of both: the historical record contains ample evidence that technology destroys work skills and creates work skills, reduces employment and creates employment, contributes to pollution and provides instruments, chemicals and other means for the reduction of pollution, disrupts established lifestyles, social and economic processes, forms of organisation, and established relationships amongst individuals and between individuals and institutions in society, industry and governments, and causes the creation of new lifestyles, new social and business organisations, new relationships, and oftentimes even new elements in language. The question is what happens on balance, and what measures are taken to minimise the negative effects on individuals and society at large. In the assessment, it is not enough to show that more skills are created than destroyed, more employment is created in the long run than reduced in the short run, or that technology contributed more to the reduction of pollution than to the creation of pollution. If technology contributes to a general increase in economic and social welfare, then economic equity and social justice dictate that those who are adversely effected by it be given a share of the increment in general welfare. After all, the increase in general welfare has been obtained at their expense.

This does not mean, of course, that society should tolerate any negative effects as long as those effected negatively are adequately compensated. There are potential negative effects to human life and nature from radiation, for example, which cannot be counter-balanced by compensatory arrangements. In such cases, unless alternative processes are found which eliminate the negative effects, the technology must be adjudged socially unacceptable. The consideration of *efficiency* without the *cost of efficiency* neglects an important aspect of net economic and social welfare; and the consideration of *efficiency* without *equity* neglects an important aspect of the economic and social purpose of enterprise.

These issues suggest a need for social control of enterprise, and raise the question of how much public agency supervision and control can be exercised without impeding technological progress. Society at large appears favourably disposed towards the scientific community in research and experimentation, but it is not similarly disposed towards the industrial community. It is perhaps a matter of perceived purpose: the scientific community is deemed to be in quest of knowledge; while the industrial community is perceived to be in quest of profit.

Often, it is difficult for society to decide in advance on the nature of effects that are likely to emanate from experimental processes, and it must rely on the ethical standards of the scientific community for protection. The agitation about genetic engineering is a good example: the potential for social terror, vividly demonstrated on television with the exploits of human clones, caused concern even within the scientific community. But, that aspect of the process was an experimental possibility, which contains a potential for immeasurable good. The field of biotechnology which is an offshot of this process of experimentation promises very significant benefits for humankind. The agitation and media exaggeration about experimental possibilities was not without benefit: the scientific community itself was caused to pause and examine its moral responsibility.

The Purpose of Technology

What is the purpose of technology? It cannot be an end in itself. It must be a means to the attainment of some goals, to the solution of some problems in society and the economy: to produce goods and services which cannot be produced without technology; to produce more goods and services; to produce some goods and services more efficiently; to reduce the social and economic costs associated with the production of some goods and services. To paraphrase Harvard University's Harvey Brooks, technology may not solve all of our problems, but our problems cannot possibly be solved without the introduction of new technology.[2]

All nations, rich and poor, developed and developing, capitalist, socialist, communist, face four realities: *scarcity* of human and material resources: *inefficiency* in the allocation and utilisation of their scarce resources; insufficient *predictability* in the outcomes of economic and social activity; and inadequate *control* over economic and social processes.

The first two are related, and technology has been applied successfully to the alleviation of the problems inherent in them. *Scarcity* of human and material resources imposes limitations on what individual countries can produce, how much they can produce, where production will take place, and when. Libya has the oil but not the specialised human resources; India has the specialised human resources, but not the capital and natural resources; Japan has an educated labour force, capital, and high level technology, but limited natural resources; while the United States seems to have more of everything than any other country, yet experiences greater difficulties in the efficient utilisation of its human and natural resources than the many countries who have less. Technology alleviates the constraints imposed by scarcity through increased *efficiency* – by making it possible to produce more with the same scarce resources: putting an instrument in the hands of a worker, enables the worker to produce more; putting a more efficient instrument in the hands of the same worker, enables the worker to produce even more; fertilising a parcel of scarce land will increase its output; applying capital equipment in the cultivation of that parcel will increase its output even more; an engineer will produce more and better work, if some of the complex calculations involved in his work were to be performed faster and more reliably; and the physician will attend to more patients, and provide more reliable service, if some of the diagnostic work were to be performed more efficiently and more reliably. Computer technology increases the efficiency of the engineer; while the same technology, combined with laboratory and X-ray technology, increases the efficiency of the physician. In short, technology relaxes the constraints on production imposed by scarcity of resources, and increases the production possibilities beyond what they would be in its absence. As the British economist Professor John Hicks put it: 'Every change in technology displaces the production frontier . . . every gain in technical knowledge displaces it outwards.[3] By enabling scarce resources to produce more, technology has an effect similar to that of an increase in supply of the scarce resources. If constraints prevent an increase in the supply of doctors, for example, an increase in supply of complementary equipment, which enables the available supply of doctors to attend more patients will have the same effect as if the supply of doctors were increased. The production frontier will be pushed outward.

Computers and telecommunications technology are expected to increase the efficiency in allocation of scarce consumer resources as well. By making information on comparative prices, qualities, terms and conditions of use, locations and other, readily available, the consumer will be enabled to make more rational choices. Indeed, given such information in advance of embarking on the marketing expeditions, consumers will be able to make their decision choices at home, carry out the relevant calculations, and proceed directly to the sources of their choices. Such a possibility will not only make the choices more rational, but will also reduce the cost of search.

Allocative efficiency is also expected in labour markets. Readily available information on where the jobs are, the terms and conditions of employment in different industries, the social and institutional conditions – schools, housing, recreational facilities – that prevail in different localities, and readily available information on where the workers are, their ages, skills, and work experiences, will increase the efficiency in the allocation of human resources, and reduce the considerable costs involved in workers searching for jobs and employers searching for workers.

Technology, particularly electronic technology, is said to provide the best hope for grappling successfully with the other two realities – *predictability* and *control* of economic and social processes. A measure of progress has been recorded in relation to control, and more is confidently expected: electronic sensors have achieved a measure of control over industrial processes; the operational efficiency of many consumer durables has been brought under control by that same technology; and it is generally expected that computers and microelectronic technology will facilitate greater quality control and improve the process of inventory control.

Predictability is a different matter: the outcomes of most critical processes – national budgets, inflation, productivity, the weather, maintenance of health – are influenced by so many variables as to make it almost impossible to predict with any reasonable degree of accuracy. Policy-measures reasonably effective in one country have proven less effective in another, even though similarly structured; and policy-measures reasonably effective in one period have proven ineffective in another. All the electronic sophistication introduced in recent years in the measurement of changes in industry employment, occupations, prices, the rate of economic growth, the weather, does not seem to have improved the predictability over the more primitive methods used in the past. Indeed, rumour has it that in relation to weather forecasting, the North American Indian's method of wetting an index finger and holding it up to the elements, or smelling the chillness of the air, produced greater accuracy than satellite communication and computer analysis. The problem remains critical. In an era of rapid communication, when information is generated and disseminated rapidly, there is an expectation that decisions will be taken rapidly. The continuing uncertainty in outcomes inherent in deficient predictability, impair the decision-making process. So far, sophisticated technology has made it possible to carry out complex calculations, which, in turn, have facilitated a cop-out system of imperfect predictability, usually presented in the form of a number of 'scenarios.' In 'scenario one', the outcome will likely be such; in 'scenario two', the outcome will be the such, plus–minus something; 'scenario three', the such plus–minus something will be different. Take your pick, and you will likely be as close to the correct outcome as any of the other picks. There is progress, but it is very slow; and in this slowness society finds hope for the minimisation of pain in transitional adjustment.

The Nature of Technological Change

Technological changes – computers, chips, robots, fibre optics and other materials, word processors – are applications of ideas to production processes. The ideas may relate to new products or improvements to existing products; new machinery or improvements to existing machinery; new organisational structures or changes in the organisation of production; and to scores of other activities and processes. The emphasis is on the application of knowledge, not on additions to knowledge. Additions to the stock of knowledge or modifications of it, may be mere inventions; inventions must be technically and economically feasible to be transformed into innovations, and applied to production processes. Inventions that are not technically and economically feasible remain good ideas that could not find application. All new ideas do not become inventions; and all inventions do not become innovations.

Another characteristic of technological change is that it is continuous: the application of one idea generates another, which, in turn, becomes the basis for another. It is a continuum of ideas that finds application in production processes.[4] And because of this continuity, it is often very difficult to establish cause and effect in the outcomes. For example, Adam Smith saw in the division of labour a cause and effect relationship with technology, in the sense that the division of labour made it necessary to produce complementary technical instruments to increase the efficiency of labour, and the technical instruments dictated, in turn, that labour acquire the necessary skills to use the instruments efficiently. Which was the cause and which the effect is difficult to say. The two are interrelated.

Interrelatedness is a reality that permeates through production processes and society at large: existing processes in the economy and society suggest potential changes in instruments of production, the organisation of processes, in products and services; in response, new instruments, products and processes replace old instruments, products and processes, which, in turn, dictate changes in lifestyles, in work functions, in inter-personal relationships, and make it necessary that producers, distributors and users as well, acquire new knowledge. Consider any innovation, however insignificant it may seem, and trace its effects from producers, through distributors, to consumers and society at large. At the very beginning the people who generate the idea are involved; then there are the people who decide whether the idea is to be pursued; they are followed by the designers, the builders of models and the testers; there are then the designers and creators of the machinery and equipment needed for the production of the innovation; followed by the installation of the production processes, the training of labour, the purchase of materials, the establishment of distribution networks, and provisions for servicing the innovation. In addition, at all levels of the process, transportation services, financial services, and various public services are usually involved. The user, whether user in production or user in consumption, sees only the final product – the pocket calculator, the word-processor, the copier, the microwave oven, or the coffee-maker – and becomes aware of what it displaces and what immediate effects it has. The actual effects are much more widespread.

Awareness of all effects is a necessary condition for the understanding and evaluation of the implications of technological change. It effects both the supply side and the demand side of the market. It effects the demand side through the introduction of new products, which change consumer preferences and the patterns of demand; and it effects the supply side by changing the ways in which scarce resources are used. The effects at the user level – whether it is the producer-user or the consumer-user level – are often only a fraction of the effects on the economy and society at large.[5]

Another reality of technological development is that it is not a closed-end process; it is open ended and continuous. Small technical changes are an almost biological phenomenon, and like adjustments to biological changes most economic and social adjustments are almost automatic and routine. From time to time some radically different change takes place, dictating radical adjustments, but in most such instances the changes are applied over sufficiently long periods to allow for reasonably smooth adjustments in economic (including employment) and social processes. Newcomer produced a steam engine in 1712; James Watt worked on it in 1763 to repair and improve its performance; Matthew Boulton with Watt's technical expertise started to manufacture it in 1785. It took 73 years from initial introduction to widespread use. The computer has taken 30 years, so far, and perhaps it will take another 30 before its full potential is utilised in integrative processes. In the past 30 years we have been inundated with fictional scenarios of imminent production processes which will require no human intervention or assistance. The reality to-date has been neither imminent nor humanless. The scenarios have turned out to be sandcastles without foundations and without cementing elements – the sandcastles of children playing on the beach, built on fantasy models, without the real elements of lasting construction. The changes have not been as widespread as projected; social and economic processes have adjusted without any traumatic effects; and all indications are that the technological changes, and the responsive changes in economic and social processes will continue to take place at mutually accomodative rates.

Impact on the Organisation of Work

It is a technological imperative, supported by the historical reality, that the structure of industrial organisations and the organisation of work processes are substantially dictated by the nature of technology in operation.[6] The productive capacity of capital equipment dictates the size of production processes: large scale equipment dictates large scale operations and large scale operations dictate large organisations. What processes and organisations will emerge from the application of microelectronic technology? The convergence of computers and telecommunications technologies into integrated networks would suggest large scale operations and very large organisations. On the other hand, easy access to information on products, processes, and prices may lead to decentralisation.

The technological infrastructure will be radically different from the electromechanical infrastructure in existence at present, and will cause radical changes in the organisation of work processes in factories and offices, in shops and classrooms, in hospitals and financial institutions, at home and everywhere. Indeed, with the gradual integration of computer and telecommunications systems, the computer created infrastructure in effect at present will itself change radically, and the computer-related work processes in effect currently will themselves change significantly.

We have a reasonably good understanding of what will be possible with the convergent computer–telecommunications systems; it is not yet clear what kinds of modifications will be necessary to reduce their negative effects on individuals and society at large. Some aspects of the emerging systems may not be compatible with human capacities; others may not meet legal requirements; and still others may be incompatible with efficient methods of management. We know, for example, that information will be centralised, access to it will be easy and instantaneous, and the transmission of information will speed-up significantly. We also know that the settlement of commercial transactions will take place instantaneously – upon completion of the transaction the respective accounts will be credited and debited, regardless of the part in the world where the transactions take palce; we will search the stocks of libraries and shops from home; and we will access via the television set up-to-the-minute information on health care, education, travel (with pictures and prices), finance, employment opportunities, and almost anything else. In relation to work activities, it will be possible to input the system from wherever it can be accessed, at any time of day or night, and it will be equally possible to request outputs relevant to the work activity. But, there are implications in all this which create uncertainties and provide the basis for fictional scenarios like those in Orwell's 1984: who will get access to the information? Who will have control over the information? How much information will be deposited into the system? What are the legal implications? Should there be an official audit process? How much should the system be allowed to do?

These are important questions; but they are not yet a source of concern. The concerns are related to the efficient use of computer systems: the organisation of appropriate production processes; imperfections on the input side of systems; imperfections in dissemination and use of system outputs; software imperfections; and equipment incompatibilities causing costly down-times. A particularly critical imperfection to which frequent reference is made is the inadequate and often imperfect feedback from users of computer outputs. Whether these are work process imperfections, system imperfections, or manifestations of resistance to the new technology, remains to be determined. Nevertheless, it is noteworthy that through most of the 30 years over which computer technology has been used extensively in production processes, productivity in the economy at large has been down. Since the technology is supposed to increase efficiency, does the decline in productivity mean inefficient use? Is it possible that the information that is being produced is inadequate or inappropriate for decision-making purposes? Is it possible that work processes are so imperfect as to neutralise the potential efficiency of the system? Is it possible that management is not yet accustomed to the efficient use of the information that is provided? Is it possible that, like most of the television use, the systems are being put to superficial uses?

All these questions on the nature of activities to which computers are being put, the nature of activities to which they may be put, the constraints, inefficiencies and imperfections, are a manifestation of the fact that the technology is still at a transitional phase. The organisation of work processes that emerges from a technological infrastructure dominated by an interactive computer and telecommunications system range from the pedestrian (the existing system with minor modifications) to the utopian.

Employment Effects of Technology

In 1949, the person credited with the fundamentals of computer logic predicted 'a decade or more of ruin and despair'. Automation was going to abolish jobs at an unprecedented rate, and was to create mass unemployment.[7] The decade went by, and instead of mass unemployment, employment in the United States increased from 58 million in

1949 to 65 million in 1959; another decade went by, and employment increased by another 13 million to 78 million in 1969; and then another decade went by, and employment increased by 18 million to 96 million in 1979. What can one say about such forecasts, except that they are usually made by people whose understanding of how the economy works is very limited? The reality of economic processes on the aggregate is much different from the 'logic' underlying an extrapolation from a single development, even when that development, like the advent of microelectronic technology, has pervasive characteristics. Care must be exercised to not generalise on the basis of limited premises, and to guard against the possibility of the fallacy of composition, to which reference was made earlier.

Predictions of substantial future involuntary unemployment are generally based on actual and expected reductions in the labour intensity of *existing* production processes, within *existing* organisational systems, and within the limitations of *existing* ranges of occupational work functions. For reasons which relate largely to the pervasiveness of microelectronic technology, and the expected extraordinary increase in productive capacities of processes utilising microelectronic instruments, the historical employment creation effect of technological change is either disregarded or significantly minimised.

It is important that these assumptions and limitations be borne in mind when confronted with predictions of pending unemployment, for they make the difference between future reality and future fiction. Considering that all production processes tend to reduce their labour intensities over time, it is not difficult to demonstrate an outcome of excessive unemployment under the assumption that the new processes and expansion in processes, will generate only limited new employment.

To-date the impact of microelectronic instruments and processes on employment appears to have been positive. On the whole, more jobs have been created than eliminated. There is no evidence of negative effects in employment related to accounting and finance, which is an area of employment most affected by data processing; there is no evidence of negative effects in office employment generally, which is an area of employment most effected by the application of electronic office equipment; nor is there any evidence of negative employment effects in other areas of activity where computers and computer-related processes are known to have been applied extensively such as banking, finance, insurance and real estate, research activities, warehousing and different manufacturing activities.

Perhaps two developments account for the absence of negative effects to-date: one is that microelectronic instruments and processes have been used largely in the production of services which could not have been produced by conventional methods. In a sense they become complementary to the existing systems of production. The typewriter continues to be used for the typing function, while the word processor complements the production process with its capacity for storage of information, editing, and changes in the organisation of typed work without re-typing. To the extent that this is the case, microelectronic instruments and processes are used parallel to conventional processes – they broaden the conventional processes. A number of studies have reported a broadening in the range of work activities as a result of the introduction of microelectronic technology.[8] The second development accounting for the absence of negative effects is the still limited scope of inter-establishment microelectronic communication links. This means that regardless how extensive a microelectronic system an establishment may have for its own internal purposes, as long as its system is not linked with the systems of other establishments it would have to maintain a conventional system for communication with other establishments. In other words, an establishment may have electronic mail within its operations, but as long as its electronic system is not linked to the system of other enterprises, communication with them will continue to be by letter and telephone, which dictates the maintenance of the conventional system for external communication.

Predictions that technology – computers, microprocessors, robots, word processors, communications technology, and whatever – will cause massive unemployment are based upon two related premises: one is that technology makes it possible to produce *more of the goods and services that are being produced* with less and less human labour; and the other is that demand *for those* goods and services will fall short of the technical capacity of the economy to produce them. Both premises are valid. But, they are valid in relation to the goods and services that were being produced by the technology that is being displaced, notwithstanding whether those goods and services are exactly the same or in modified forms. They are not valid in relation to new goods and services produced by the new technology; not valid in relation to new processes of production *and distribution* induced by the new technology; and not valid in relation to goods and services generally. In other words, they are valid in relation to the replacement of a typewriter with a word processor, or in relation to the replacement of metal pipes with plastic pipes; but they are not valid in relation to office and office-related services generally, and they are not valid in relation to the construction industry generally. Furthermore, even if it should happen that they were valid in relation to the industries in which the technologies were applied, compensating goods and services in other industries will render them invalid on the aggregate.

The validity of the two premises in relation to employment generally, depends on the rate of increase in demand for goods and services. There is no dispute over the reality that goods and services are being produced in larger and larger quantities with less and less labour – tons of steel, numbers of automobiles, bushels of wheat, typewritten pages, and whatever. The dispute is on whether this reality will cause general unemployment. The historical record tells us that technology has tended to not only increase the capacity to produce more, but also increased incomes and facilitated the production of different goods and services. The labour not used in the production of existing goods and services, in wheat production for example, became employed in the production of the emerging goods and services – tractors and combines for example.

Another relevant reality that warrants a brief comment in this introduction relates to the sources of demand for goods and services: references to the nature and variety of goods and services available on the market, and the possible rate of increase in demand for them, are usually made in terms of what and how much people are able and willing to buy. Concerns are expressed that consumer needs are becoming satiated, and that another car, another television set, and another whatever, will not be enough to sustain the increase in demand that would be necessary to employ fully the rapidly expanding productive capacity of the economy. Such concerns are not founded on reality: 90 per cent of the world's population barely satisfy their basic needs; they are far from satiation. Also, the evidence from countries which have achieved high living standards suggests that consumer wants are expansive – more things, new things, different things. And account must be taken of the fact that the purchasing power at the disposal of consumers, and consumer preferences, do not determine the total of goods and services that will be produced. Large quantities of goods and services are produced for, and purchased by governments – federal, state and local – for their own use and for the people at large – for the military, for space exploration, for road-building, for education and health, for parks and recreation, and hundreds of other activities; and large quantities of goods and services are produced for other countries. It is true that many goods and services purchased in a country were produced in other countries, and when employment effects are considered account must be taken of what happens on balance – the jobs that are created in the production of goods and services sold in other countries, against the jobs that are lost by the purchase of goods and services produced in other countries. But, the important point is that it is wrong, it is limiting, to view the demand for goods and services in terms of what and how much the people are able and willing to buy. The total demand, from all sources, must be considered.

Computers and computer-related technologies are still in transition. As a result, it is not yet perfectly clear what effects they will have on the division of labour, on participation in work activities, on the organisation of production processes – on the shop floor, in the office, at the administrative level – and on the distribution of employment amongst industrial, commercial and institutional activities. We know significant changes are in the offing, and we also know that the transitional nature of the new technology makes the present effects transitional. We will not know the ultimate nature and extent of the effects until the technologies stabilise somewhat. For example, a few steps have been taken towards the electronisation of office work: computers, word processors and peripherals of all sorts have been introduced; in some places these have been linked together into integrated systems, and in other have been used independently of one another. In places where integrated systems are operational, participants communicate with one another electronically, and access information on their desk-top videoscreens directly. But, that is all. Organisational structures, processes of work and work relationships have not changed as much as one would expect from such systems. The explanation for this will be found in the fact that the application of the technologies is still limited to processes and communication within individual firms only. The full impact, which will be considerable, will not come until the systems of firms and institutions are linked together into interactive networks – until the system of each enterprise is linked to the systems of banks and other financial institutions, with the systems of their suppliers, with the systems of transportation companies, and with the systems of their customers, whether the customers are other enterprises or customer intermediaries, such as retail establishments. When such *telematic*[9] networks come into effect, radical changes will take place in every aspect of people-work relationships: forecasts of fictional changes and impacts abound; reality will be different; certainly the organisation of work will change; the nature of work will change; and the distribution of employment amongst industries and occupations will change. In what ways, how much, and where, are the issues examined in the chapters that follow.

Are Concerns about Employment Justified?

History is replete with examples of resistance to technological changes because of concerns about their economic consequences: the government of the city of Danzig had the inventor of the ribbon loom secretly strangled, because of concerns about its effect on employment in the city; and Arkwright's cotton spinning machine was opposed by both spinners and landlords, the first from fear of unemployment, and the second from concerns that they may have to pay higher taxes for relief if spinners were to be thrown out of work.[10]

Changes in technology do affect employment: machinery and equipment are introduced in processes of production where the work is performed largely by people; new production materials are introduced which reduce the time it takes to produce a unit of output; and new machinery and equipment is introduced which produces more per unit of time than the old machinery and equipment. The machine washing clothes, the machine washing dishes, and the automation of filing in offices are examples of the first; the replacement of metal pipes with plastic pipes in construction, and the use of electronic parts instead of electro-mechanical parts in calculators, copying machines, and telex machines, are examples of the second; and the replacement of mechanical calculators with electronic calculators, and of typewriters with word processors are examples of the third. All of these affect the employment of people, and the nature of work functions people perform.

But, these are not new developments: such changes have taken place throughout history. It is true that the current wave of technological change is radically different from past waves,[11] and some of the changes may be faster than previous major changes, but they must be examined from the standpoint of their impact of society at large, not from the standpoint of their nature and rate. Societies have different capacities to absorb change, depending on the extent to which they are accustomed to change. The current concern does not appear to be related so much to the nature and rate of the technological change as to its appropriateness for work activities performed in service industries, which employ much of the labour force. It is feared that if services-producing processes were to become as capital intensive as goods-producing processes have become, it will not be possible to find employment for all who want to work.

Furthermore, radical changes in technology call for radical changes in production processes, knowledge and skills; and the rate at which changes take place has significant implications for the adjustment process – the time needed for the re-education, retraining and relocation of the labour force, and the time that is necessary for adjustments in society and the economy. The historical record is not a useful guide here, except perhaps to show the elements that contributed to successful and unsuccessful adjustments. The relationship between the nature of change, the rate of change, and adjustments in processes, employment, occupations, society and the economy, suggests that the implications must be examined in the context of the social conditions that prevail when the changes take place – the technical and scientific sophistication of the population at large, the general level of education, and the nature of production processes. In the context of differences in social conditions, the simple mechanical implements introduced in the early periods of the industrial revolution may well have had more devastating effects on production processes, employment and skills, than can be expected from the highly sophisticated computer and telecommunications technology that is being introduced today. The more appropriate the social conditions and the economic infrastructure for a given technological change, the lesser are likely to be the negative effects. Which means that the appropriateness of social and economic conditions will tend to have a neutralising effect on the potential negative consequences.

The relationship between technology and employment can be looked at as one of *displacement* and *replacement*: workers are displaced from some processes and replaced by workers in other processes. Often the same workers are involved in the change, which is in essence self-replacement. Workers displaced from the horse-drawn carriage industry were replaced by workers in the automobile industry; workers displaced from work activities related to the attendance of horses were replaced by workers employed at gasoline stations; and workers displaced from repair and maintenance of saddles and carriages were replaced by automobile mechanics and maintenance workers. Imbalances in the displacement–replacement adjustment process are usually associated with different rates of displacement and replacement in the respective industries and related processes throughout the economy; the nature of skills that are being displaced and the nature of those that are being replaced; the training and retraining programmes available; the capacities of displaced workers for retraining; and the general state of the economy during the period of change.

One of the major displacements in employment in recent years was caused by the substitution of dial telephones for manual (operator directed) services. Thousands of telephone operators were displaced. But, there was no significant outcry. Other activities in the telephone industry were expanding rapidly, and the period coincided with general economic expansion and growth in employment. Replacement was relatively easy. More recent changes in the same industry produced considerable agitation, even though the number of workers affected was nowhere close to the number of operators that were displaced. But, a different class of workers is now involved, and economic conditions have been different: the affected workers are predominantly tradesmen, with limited alternative opportunities; and economic conditions generally are characterised by limited growth and excessive involuntary unemployment.

Successful accommodation to a major phase of technological change requires a prolonged period of sustained economic growth. Frequent periods of expansion and contraction of short duration are disruptive to the adjustment process, particularly when retraining, relocation and re-employment are involved. There is nothing less demoralising than to retrain a worker and not be able to place in employment on completion of the retraining programme, or to move a worker to a new job, in a new community, and have that worker laid off shortly after re-employment. These are the causes of agitation, not the technological changes.

Advocates of technological change would argue that technological changes cause displacement and replacement; destroy and create; they do not cause unemployment. To the extent that some people become and remain unemployed for long, the causes will be found in inadequate training facilities and programmes, inability or lack of desire on the part of workers to move, preferences for work that is not available, and inadequate demand relative to the productive capacity of the economy. Concerns should be directed to these causes and not towards technological changes. This line of argument would suggest that the government of the city of Danzig should have directed its attention to programmes designed to accommodate the technological progress, rather than to ways designed to dispose of the inventor.

2 Evolution, Revolution and Manpower Adjustments

The Electronic 'Revolution'

References to on-going or pending technological revolutions, and to on-going and pending microelectronic, telematic or whatever electronic revolutions, are intended to draw attention not so much to the technologies themselves, as to their potential for revolutionary consequences for work, working, worker–employer relationships, the organisation of processes of production, and generally for the nature and structure of social and economic existence. It is analogous to a political revolution where the government is the instrument, and the revolutionary changes are the changes in established economic, political and social relationships.

In the evolution of industrialism, the machine was the instrument that initiated the revolutionary process; the factory system of production initiated revolutionary changes in the organisation of economic and social processes; and the industrial system revolutionised the economy and society at large. A machine does not by itself make a factory; and a factory does not by itself make an industrial system. Scores of interrelated processes and functional activities must be in place to turn a machine into a factory, and factories into an industrial system. The same applies to the evolution of the electronic system: individual electronic instruments, whether they be computers, word processors, printers or whatever, do not make an integrated electronic process; and an integrated electronic process within an enterprise does not make an electronic system. The advent of the computer, like the advent of the first machine, initiated a revolutionary process; and the integration of different electronic instruments into continuous production processes is initiating revolutionary changes in the organisation of economic and social processes; when the integrated electronic processes of individual enterprises – commercial, industrial and institutional enterprises – are linked together into an electronic system, the revolutionary process will be completed. The industrial infrastructure initiated by the machine more than 200 years ago will be replaced by an electronic infrastructure initiated by the computer. But, for such a system to come into being a large number of inter-related technological, social and economic conditions must evolve.

In 1769 Arkwright patented the water frame, and James Watt patented the steam engine. In themselves these were revolutionary capital instruments. But, the economic revolution which they initiated did not take effect until decades later – until complementary instruments and appropriate work processes made possible the establishment of the factory system.[1] The water frame and the steam engine were in use for a long period before the introduction of the factory system, not unlike the use of computers over the past 30 years. But the revolutionary impact was not felt in society at large until their convergence with other instruments into integrated factory systems. It was then that the machine system destroyed the handicraft system, and the factory system of production destroyed the domestic (cottage) system. The revolution was in the organisation of production processes, and in the relationship between production processes and the people as participants in the production processes. A similar development should be anticipated in the evolution of electronic technology: the revolutionary effect will not come into full force until computers, computer-related instruments and telecommunications technology become integrated into production systems and change radically the organisation of production processes.

The industrial revolution, to which frequent references are made as a process of economic change, and to which a time period is usually assigned, stretched over more than a century in the country of origin. Initially, machine production was introduced piecemeal, not unlike the introduction of computers over the past thirty years and word processors over the past ten years, without any concerted effort to determine the ultimate effects on workers, working conditions, employment, and society at large. But, over time, lower equipment prices, greater knowledge on what the machines could do, increase in supply of appropriate manpower for their operation and maintenance, and increasing integration of machinery and equipment into factory systems, accelerated the rate of adoptions. By then it was too late to prevent the massive negative consequences for employment, working conditions and society at large. The owners of the capital equipment sought a return to their investment, and in quest of that introduced work schedules which ensured its continuous operation. A Factories Commission reported in 1833: 'In order to regain the time lost by stoppages, whether from the breakage of machinery, from the want of due supply of water, or from holidays, it is the custom for the people to work, sometimes half an hour, at other times an hour, and occasionally even as much as two hours daily, until the whole of the lost time is made up.'[2] Since the pay was by the day, the extra time worked was not paid. Also, to minimise the labour cost, and thereby increase the return to the capital investment, large numbers of children, seven and eight years of age, were employed. Their work and home life is described this way: 'At 4 or 5 a.m. the factory bell sounded, and half asleep they stumbled or were carried to work to begin again the unending rush . . . they came back from work too worn out that they could not eat their supper. Put to bed with food in their hands, they were found clutching it when they were roused next day.'[3] Successive Factory Acts sought to regulate the process of change and its impact, but as we are today discovering over again, when capital is sunk into a process of production, it becomes very difficult to dismantle or to alter significantly, and the work processes and consequences of its operation become imperative. Capital became the dominant factor, and all effects associated with its operation had to be accepted as a condition for its operation. Constraints on its operation would effect the return negatively and discourage further investment. The arguments have not changed much over the past 150 or so years, and public policies continue to lag dangerously behind the introduction of new technologies. History is a good teacher, but its effect is limited to those who learn from it.

Although the industrial revolution is commonly associated with machine production, it was really the introduction of energy to machine production that caused the revolutionary changes in production and organisation of work processes. The replacement of human muscle power in the operation of the machines, and the linkages of machines into production systems, brought radical changes to worker–work relationships, to interpersonal relationships in the work place, and initiated significant changes in the location and organisation of industry. The source of energy supply became a factor in industry location. A new industry (power generation) emerged, creating new investment and employment opportunities on one hand, and unemployment on the other. Over the decades that followed, handicraft processes made valiant efforts to survive in traditional ways, craftsmen emphasising their customised services in competition with industrial products, and relying on their direct and personal relationships with their customers for survival. But, power-driven machines and low-wage factory labour reduced unit costs and prices, produced a greater variety of competing products, and made products available on the market for immediate purchase. No more waiting at the craftsman's pleasure, and no longer limited to what the craftsman was able and willing to produce. The combined benefits of lower prices and access to variety gradually offset the advantages of customised services and friendly producer–consumer relations. The demise of the craftsman's shop was inevitable. The craftsman gradually faded away, replaced by product designers, machine operators, electricians, and scores of other occupations engaged in the distribution and sale of the large quantities and varieties of output that replaced the craftsman's output. This historical reality in the evolution of production processes during the period of the industrial revolution is very relevant to the on-going electronic revolution.

Significant changes in processes of production are very seldom sudden. Usually, large enterprises are the first to introduce the new processes, followed by smaller and smaller enterprises as equipment prices fall, the needed capital outlay declines, and most important of all, as the risk diminishes. Eventually, equipment proliferates in a variety of standardised forms, knowledge about it increases – what it can and cannot do, for how long and what operating and maintenance costs are involved – introduction accelerates and becomes widespread. Processes of production change, the organisation of industry changes, work functions change, new social and economic environments emerge. The power-driven machine, and the factory system that it brought about, resulted in increasing concentration of industry, and transformed the work environment from widely dispersed shop-crafts and craftsmen to concentration of large numbers of workers within the confines of individual factories.

Similar evolutionary changes are in evidence in relation to the introduction of computer technology. Initially, only large enterprises, with pools of cheap capital and capacity to take risks, such as insurance companies, invested in computer technology. Over time, as knowledge about the capacity of computers increased, as new models appeared on the market with varying production capacities, and as the range of prices widened downward, purchases accelerated. But, we are still at the phase of the machine; not yet at the phase of the system. As a result, production processes and worker-work relationships have not changed to the extent that the revolutionary nature of the technology would suggest. As long as the new technology remains largely customised, its introduction will remain limited. Standardisation of hardware and software is a key condition to widespread adoption and the change of individual processes into process systems. When that happens, radical changes will take place in work processes, the work environment, the organisation of industry, the economy and society at large.

The Evolution of Industrialism

There is little doubt that the widespread introduction of new technology, in the form of microelectronics, biotechnology and telecommunications systems will bring about radical changes in production processes. Radical changes in production processes will, in turn, effect the respective functional roles and productivities of all factors of production. The precise nature and extent of effect on each factor is difficult to establish at this stage of technological development and application. But, it may be possible to gain some understanding from an examination of the functional roles of factors under different economic settings.

Economists make reference to three factors of production: *land* (resources), *capital* (machinery, equipment, factories, offices, and other produced instruments of production); and *labour* (everyone who participates in work activity – from the chambermaid to the president). When reference is made to employment, as in the production function, the reference is to the employment of all factors, not just the labour force.

Before the introduction of capital instruments as we know them today, the capital factor was constituted of wooden implements used in agriculture and construction, small implements used by craftsmen in

TABLE 2.1 *Percentage of labour force employed in agriculture*

Country	*Population in 1977 (millions)*	*% of labour force in agriculture*	*Country*	*Population in 1977 (millions)*	*% of labour force in agriculture*
China	885.6	63	Thailand	43.8	77
India	631.7	73	Turkey	41.9	62
Indonesia	133.5	60	Egypt	37.8	51
Bangladesh	81.2	78	Ethiopia	30.1	81
Nigeria	79.0	56	Zaire	25.7	76
Pakistan	74.9	58	Tanzania	16.3	84
Vietnam	50.6	70	Afghanistan	14.3	80

SOURCE *World Development Report, 1979*, World Bank, Washington, D.C., 1979, pp. 126–7 and 162–3.

their shops, the animals that were used in work activities and for the production of milk, meats and fats, and the skills and knowledge of the people. The dominant factor of production was the land, and both labour and capital were wedded to it. Whoever controlled the land exercised control over labour and hence over the people. This continues to be the current reality in most countries. The 1979 *World Development Report* of the World Bank lists 62 countries, with two-thirds of the world's population, still employing more than 50 per cent of their people in agriculture. (see Table 2.1, p. 22.)

In industrialised countries, the proportions of the labour force employed in agriculture in 1977 ranged between 2 per cent in the United Kingdom and 21 per cent in Ireland. In the United States, 3 per cent of the labour force were employed in agriculture, in Germany and Sweden 5 per cent, in Canada, Switzerland and the Netherlands 6 per cent, in Japan 14 per cent and in France 10 per cent.

Alvin Toffler's Second Wave, which is supposed to have 'swept across the planet' and replaced the 'agricultural techno-sphere',[4] is reality to only parts of planet earth. Although all countries employ various kinds of machinery, equipment and other capital instruments, it cannot be said that all countries have in place industrial systems. The horse, the mule, the donkey and the camel, the cow, the water buffalo, men, women and children continue to be the main sources of power in most countries, and the land, the people, birds and animals continue to be the main agents and sources of subsistence. In short, most of the planet continues to ride and depend on Toffler's First Wave. To most people the Second Wave is nothing more than a sound: some of them can hear the roar, while others can only detect a distant rumble. Even countries that are today classified as industrial, did not really experience the effects of a wave-like impact from the so called industrial revolution. The industrialisation period has been so long, that it would be more accurate to characterise the effect as a ripple effect. The pebble was cast in England, and the ripple spread ever so slowly. Almost 200 years have gone by, and it continues to spread slowly.

In most countries, land continues to be the dominant factor of production. But, labour is the critical factor. Aside from its functional role in relation to land-related production processes, labour is the only factor that transmits knowledge and thereby perpetuates improvements in production processes. The generation of knowledge, and the means by which knowledge is transmitted and applied to production are key elements in the evolution of industrialism. In *land-dominated economies* knowledge is generated by the people, and becomes embodied largely in the people. It is applied by the people directly into production processes on the land, in households, and in craft shops, and passed on largely by the people from generation to generation – father to son, craftsman to journeymen, journeymen to apprentices. The knowledge becomes manifested directly into household utensils and appliances, household produced foodstuffs and clothing, in methods of land cultivation, into means of conveyance, and in other processes of production.

The production of capital instruments reduces the critical role of labour in both the application of knowledge and the transmission of knowledge: the capital instruments themselves embody the functional knowledge that they apply to production processes; they transmit that knowledge over time and from place to place through mobility; and displace from labour the corresponding knowledge. Although the generation of knowledge remains in the exclusive domain of labour, the increasing introduction of capital instruments transforms increasing proportions of the labour force into capital dependents in production processes.

In *capital-dominated economies*, most knowledge is embodied in the capital infrastructure. Advances in knowledge become embodied in new technology continuously, which means that at any point of time a modern technological infrastructure will contain all of the knowledge applicable to the respective production processes. The space shuttle and the computers and telecommunications systems to which it is linked contain most of the up-to-date knowledge on computer and telecommunications technology. Over time much of that knowledge will be transferred to other processes through electronic capital instruments, including microchips. So, unlike land dominated economies where knowledge is applied to production processes directly by the people, and transferred from generation to generation by the people, in capital dominated economies knowledge is applied to production processes largely through capital instruments, and it is transferred largely through the transfer of technology. The role of most labour becomes complementary and supportive to capital.

The subject of this book concerns the possibility of further reductions in the role of labour, as production processes become automated, and as telematic systems are introduced. The possibility is considered of removing labour entirely from the complementary and supportive relationships to capital, and the further possibility of capital undertaking the only function which heretofore has remained the domain of labour, namely, the generation of knowledge. As long as the generation of knowledge remains exclusively a human capacity, the functional capacities of automated processes and telematic systems will be limited to the nature and extent of knowledge transferred to them by the human factor. But, what if microelectronic processes were to be given the capacity to generate knowledge? What role then for labour in production processes? These are questions that will be considered in due course. They dictate more background information and more retrospective analysis before the formulation of answers.

When the role of labour is examined in relation to capital, land or specific processes of production, there is a tendency to think of the relationship in the narrow sense of one to one or one to two – worker–tractor–land or worker–tool–machine – and to project changes in this relationship to the entire economy and society. That is not, of course, what happens. A change in labour–capital relationship at the assembly line is a change at one point of a usually very long production process, involving a large number of activities and an equally large number of different factor combinations and relationships.

Production processes are linked together by an invisible organisational structure, which when operating efficiently makes each part of the system aware of developments in all other parts, and responsive to the requirements of the other parts. Failure of any of the parts to respond, whether they be suppliers of materials, suppliers of parts, public service regulatory agencies, suppliers of transportation services, distribution networks, financial institutions, or whatever, the system's efficiency will be impaired. The massive functional interdependence of processes in a system of production, distribution and use of goods and services, suggests that it is dangerous to pronounce on the possible functional relationships of the factors of production involved on the basis of changes in functional relationships at one, two, or three stages of the production process in the system. A change in the functional relationship between capital and labour at the level of the mine, at the level of the smelting process, and at the level of the transport of ore from the mine to the smelter, tells us nothing about the functional relationships at the level of engineering services, public services relating to health and safety, financial services, managerial, professional, technical and secretarial services, distributional activities, marketing activities, and many other. Specialisation in processes, and the resulting division of labour, have spread out employment over a multitude of interrelated activities.

An important characteristic of industrialism is specialisation, and an important consequence of specialisation is the emergence of markets. Both have significant implications for the spread of employment amongst wide-ranging activities. There is no market in self-sufficiency. A market emerges in response to specialisation and the resultant need for exchange – grain for fish, potatoes for corn, beans for butter, medical services for eggs. A market performs two functions: an exchange function, and an allocative function. *The exchange function* is performed at any place, in an economy where specialisation makes exchange necessary, regardless of the nature and level of development. The hunter exchanges the surplus of his kill for the surplus of the fisherman's catch. *In its allocative function* the market allocates human and material resources in the production of goods and services. Through the mechanism of the price system, a market free of government price-fixing interventions, will determine what goods and services will be produced, where, and how much, and will direct human and material resources towards the processes which will produce the indicated goods and services. References to capitalist economies as 'market' economies relate to this, the allocative function of the market, not to the exchange function. In centrally planned economies, the planning authority decides what will be produced, where, and how much, and allocates the human and material resources to the processes of production. There is no fundamental difference in the exchange functions of capitalist and noncapitalist markets: in each, the bureaucrat is paid a salary which is used to purchase the required goods and services. In essence, an exchange function.[5] A difference will be found in the methods by which the bureaucrats locate their employments, and in their respective freedoms to relocate. The bureaucrat of the capitalist system searches the market freely, and seeks the place of employment which will maximise his net advantage. He is free to respond to alternative opportunities and relocate at will. His counterpart in the Soviet Union will probably be directed to his position by some government agency, and is not as free to relocate at will. In the United States, the market allocates; in the Soviet Union, the planning authority and other government agencies do most of the allocating. In both systems, extensive minute specialisations in the production of goods and services result in extensive interdependences, which are settled in the market through exchange.

Implications for Capitalism

The widespread application of microelectronics to production and communication processes will impact significantly on economic and social organisations, structures, and processes. The structure of industry will be effected, the distribution of employment amongst sectors, industries and occupations will be effected, the nature of work will change significantly, and there are indications of an increase in government participation in the economy and society. This raises a question about the capacity of the capitalist system to adjust, particularly in relation to changes which bear on some fundamental principles of capitalism. Webster's dictionary defines capitalism as 'an economic system characterised by private or corporation ownership of capital goods, by investments that are determined by private decision rather than by state control, and by prices, production and the distribution of goods that are determined mainly in a free market'. Over the past 50 years government involvement in the economy and society has eroded the definition somewhat, but the system has remained predominantly private and the market has remained largely free. The capitalist system has adjusted successfully to the new environment. Will it adjust with equal success to the new challenge?

The renowned political economist Joseph A. Schumpeter expected the capitalist system to stagnate and eventually breakdown. He reasoned that the great economic success of the system will undermine the social institutions which protected it, and create conditions 'in which it will not be able to live'.[6] Evidently, Schumpeter did not make adequate allowance for the system's capacity to adjust. He did recognise 'the evolutionary process in capitalism',[7] but did not recognise the system's adaptability to different social institutions, and its capacity to accept, adjust and even gain vitality within a regulatory environment. Indeed, the present system would have been inconceivable as a capitalist system 50 years ago. Anyone who would have suggested the degree of government involvement presently in effect in the economy and society, would have been labelled a communist.

Technology contributed significantly to the survival and strength of the capitalist economic system. It is largely responsible for the increase in productivity, employment and incomes, and the new consumers' goods, new methods of production, the development of new markets, and new forms of industrial organisation. The creation of 'new' often involves the cost of the destruction of 'old' – in agriculture, the phasing out of horses and other draft animals and the phasing in of tractors and other equipment; in power generation, the phasing out of the water wheel, and the phasing in of generators; in logging, the phasing out of the lumberjacks and drafthorses and the phasing in of mechanical harvesters. Schumpeter called this the process of Creative Destruction.[8]

The reality of history suggests that the transformation inherent in creative destruction was beneficial to the great majority of the population. It is common to attribute to the industrial revolution all sorts of undesirable economic and social developments – economic tension, unemployment, social conflict, gulf between labour and management, unequal distribution of income. But, these undesirable developments are commonly examined in relation to some ideal rather than in relation to the reality of the economic and social systems that were replaced. It is true that the machine revolution and the factory systems that emerged from it turned a substantially independent and carefree rural workforce into a regimented industrial labour force, but it opened up opportunities for advancement and raised living standards significantly beyond what they could have ever obtained in their rural, largely land-based, economic systems. It is also true that a gulf emerged between workers and factory owners, but it was a gulf that existed before industrialisation which was given an opportunity to manifest itself. It was the concentration of large numbers of workers into factories that gave them common identities and focused on the different interests of themselves and the factory owners. Finally, it is true that independent craftsmen, who took pride in their work, were turned into indistinguishable groups of machine operators, but they too, were getting progressively better off. The industrial revolution unleashed a massive and widespread creative destruction. On balance, the undesirable social and economic developments that emerged were more than offset by the general increase in living standards of the population at large. The process of destruction was usually gradual, and afforded sufficient time for the creative processes to supplant and overcome to negative effects of the destruction. This is why capitalism survived the upheavals associated with technological change and the process of transformation.

The integration of interactive computer–communication systems involves more than production processes, products and service. It involves every aspect of economic, social and political activity – methods of inter-personal and personal–institutional communication, decision-making processes, and the making of choices. In an information society, those who control the information influence society; and those who control access to the information control participation in decision-making processes. Who will control the information? Who will allocate access to information? What criteria will be used in the determination of who will have access to what information?

Accommodating Microelectronic Processes

The world is at the threshold of a communications revolution, which will impact severely on employment and society at large. Whether the impact will be felt positively or negatively will depend on whether accommodative and adjustment mechanisms are in place and functioning efficiently in the transition from the manual/mechanical/electromechanical processes in existence heretofore, to the electronic. The transition should not be difficult, and should not cause hardships. Over the past thirty years advanced industrial economies have shifted dramatically from being predominantly goods-producing economies, to predominantly services-producing economies. The transformation into electronic/information-communication economies should be easier to accomplish from a service economy than from a goods-producing economy. The service economy has a more appropriate organisational structure, more extensive telecommunications systems, a more substantial information base, and most significantly, a more appropriate educational/occupational mix in its labour force. Given adequate time for accommodative adjustments to take effect, and given an efficient administrative process to assist with accommodative adjustments, the effect on employment and skills should not be much different from the effect recorded in the transition from a goods-producing economy to a services-producing economy.

The qualification regarding time for adjustment is critical. We do not know how long it will take the process of electronisation to become integrated into a national and international network. When that happens, utopia will become reality. Computers will then be our memory. They will be our messengers, will receive information for us and give out information on request, will advise us on the most efficient ways to do things, will keep our income and expenditure accounts, do our income tax returns, pay our bills on the indicated due dates through our bank accounts, diagnose our illnesses and indicate appropriate medications, inform us on legal decisions relevant to our problems, order groceries, and remind us of things to do.

The implication of such a microelectronic telecommunications network is so potentially disruptive to present-day work processes, interpersonal relations, social organisation and lifestyles, as to suggest a very cautious imperative: the pace of development should not be accelerated beyond the capacities of the people, institutions, the economic infrastructure, and the governing processes to adjust.

A number of major studies on the future have been published in recent years by the United Nations, the Worldwatch Institute, the World Bank, the International Union for the Conservation of Nature, the Club of Rome, and by a group appointed to respond to a request by President Carter of the US, which produced the Global 2000 Report. All reports have been highly controversial, which should not be surprising considering the nature of the subject. Predicting the nature of the future is a very difficult task: one can be scientific and extrapolate from past trends, on the assumption that trends will be approximately the same, and be criticised for a simplistic assumption; or one can be brave and disregard past trends, in which case observations and deductions become the basis of prediction.

Generally, predictions of developments in the distant future have been off the mark; and the main reason for this will be found in the premises on which the predictions are founded. Since the future environment is not known, the assessment of developments is necessarily based on some premises that are in effect at the present. But, the reality of today is history tomorrow. Therefore, whatever we say about tomorrow that is based on the reality of today must be taken as nothing more than a possibility, not as a reality. For example, the proposition is put forth that microelectronic technology will make it possible to increase productivity substantially faster than the increase in demand for goods and services, and that in the circumstances of a continuing increase in the labour force, however that is defined, unemployment will increase significantly. This prediction is based on the premise that lifestyles will remain as they are today, that work as we know it today will remain the same in future, that hours of work and their relationship to work activity will remain the same, and so on. None of these premises is valid; and the judge of that is historical reality. Who would have thought fifty years ago that only about 3 per cent of the labour force of the United States will be employed in the agricultural sector of the economy; that more than one-half of the labour force will be employed in clerical activities, retail activities, education, health, public administration and other service activities; and that only about 20 per cent of the total labour force will produce the entire volume of goods in the economy – the products of agriculture, mines, forests, and manufacturing? Who would have predicted that the hours of work would fall by one-third, that four weeks paid holiday will become almost standard fare, and that after statutory holidays, annual holidays and other times off, the average time worked per week will actually be 32 hours in 1980? Only a short decade ago we were arguing, and could not agree on the evidence that the participation of women in the labour force was increasing.

It is a reality of the future that the future will be very different from the present. Today is different from yesterday, and tomorrow will be different from yesterday and today. Many of the things that emerged today we did not anticipate yesterday; and many of the developments of tomorrow we cannot predict today. If we were to examine the details of today, in terms of the goods and services that are available, the work activities in which people are engaged, the nature of lifestyles of individuals and families, and were to compare them with a year ago, we would find very significant differences, most of which were not anticipated. Who can tell what industries will emerge from the silicone chip, the laser beam, fusion power, satelites, and what organisational systems will be brought about by robotised production processes and integrated electronic office systems?

Predictions are necessarily based on all kinds of assumptions, which, in turn, are based on conclusions about the net result of interacting developments. Since a multitude of developments can influence individual issues, some of them with positive effects and some with negative effects, it is the task of the predictor to determine the nature and significance of the net effect.

The inability to predict the future in detail suggests positive and negative implications: on the negative side is our inability to prepare in advance for change so that adjustments to change can be less painful; on the positive side it suggests that change is continuous, partly responsive to, and the result of change itself, and partly accommodative to change. This is encouraging for individuals and society at large, for it suggests that the future cannot be like the past; and since only a minority of the people at large would favour repetition of the past, future change contains hope, future shock notwithstanding.

When references are made to the different impacts of technological changes over the historical past, it is the nature of the change that it is highlighted, not the rate of it. The rate at which machine production came into being during the industrial revolution was very slow indeed; but its impact was severe because the production system to that point relied entirely on human and animal labour – all knowledge was embodied in human labour, and all power was derived from human and animal labour. The advent of machines transferred power from humans to machines, and the advent of power transferred power from humans and animals to machines. The transfer of knowledge eroded human knowledge of hand skills and processes; and the transfer of power reduced the need for human and animal power. In addition, the combined effect of machine and power on output was to increase it substantially, which in short-run periods oftentimes exceeded the capacity of the market to absorb. The impact on employment and skills was severe; but it was an impact of the nature of change, not an impact of the rate of change.

The long-run outcome suggested by the historical record is encouraging, even though some short-run effects have been negative from time to time, and from change to change. Generally, work-time has fallen and leisure-time has increased; and an hour's work has brought forth progressively more food, clothing, shelter, health care, education, and other benefits. The benefits of change have exceeded by far the costs of change. This reality notwithstanding, it is not unreasonable to retort, as has been done, 'try and tell that to workers who lost their skills, to those who lost their employment, and to those who were forced to relocate for employment'. But, such a retort, which is common amongst those concerned with the negative effects of change, merely suggests that appropriate programmes should exist to deal effectively with the negative effects. No one suggests, not even workers who are potential victims to change, that changes which entail negative effects should not take place. It suggests rather that measures and programmes should be in place to reduce, and where possible neutralise the negative effects. No change is so sudden as to preclude the planning of appropriate programmes for the reduction or neutralisation of individual and social costs.

Manpower Adjustments

Reports on manpower adjustments to technological change indicate that most workers adapt to minor innovations as easily and successfully as do new workers brought in from the external labour market.[9] Normally, the engineers and supervisors who become knowledgeable of the new technology during the planning, production and installation stages, provide some training in operational fundamentals, and then allow operators to develop their skills to the requirements of the new technology. Even where the new technology is a fully automated process, requiring of operatives the observation of signals and the pressing of certain keys, the knowledgeable engineer–supervisor is limited in his instructional function to the presentation of signals, signs and fundamentals: the operatives' effectiveness and efficiency in performance of tasks will be developed by the operatives themselves.

In most situations, the effects of technological changes on manpower are akin to plant expansion, and the adjustments required of labour in such instances are akin to in-plant relocation amongst departments and jobs.[10] The work-knowledge required by transferred workers is commonly acquired through instruction by supervisors initially, and thereafter workers become teachers of workers. *Therefore to the extent that technological changes are extensions of existing processes* the majority of workers can be expected to be able to acquire the additional work-knowledge required without undue difficulty.

Adjustment difficulties are commonly encountered when technological changes involve a significant jump in technology. In such instances workers may require some *fundamental* scientific knowledge – theoretical or/and technical – that is different from that which they possess. For example, the nature of mathematical principles required for mechanical operations are fundamentally different from those required for electronic operations. Hence, technicians knowledgeable in mechanical and electromechanical operations, will require a change in their fundamental mathematical knowledge, if they are to become knowledgeable about electronic operations.

Adjustment difficulties do not appear to arise where skills can be transferred, in whole or in part, from one process to another, and where the adjustment process involves the addition of new knowledge unto existing knowledge. Difficulties arise where existing skills cannot be readily utilised in the new processes, and where the new knowledge is not a continuation or expansion of existing knowledge. That is, difficulties of adjustment arise where innovations manifest the discontinuity (the end) of a given body of knowledge, and the initiation (the beginning) of a new body of knowledge. In such instances there cannot be a transfer of knowledge and skills; acquisition of the new knowledge and skills is necessary, and that process often requires a beginning from the beginning – the acquisition of new fundamental principles, which often means back to the classroom.

Most establishments with technologically advanced processes appear to have a variety of formal and informal educational and training programmes for their personnel: some of these relate to ongoing work functions which workers would have to perform upon transfer; some relate to equipment whose installation is pending; and some involve higher level knowledge and are used as screening processes for the selection of personnel for promotion.

The impact of electronic instruments and processes on workers involved with them has eased significantly since their initial introduction. The apprehensions associated with the need to acquire new knowledge, to master new concepts, and to gain operational proficiency with a little known technology are much less prevalent. As the revolutionary phase of the technology passed, and instruments and processes became established operationally, most subsequent 'innovations' came to be regarded as additions and improvements rather than as inventions. The prospect of adjustment to additions and improvements in technology is usually less terrifying than the prospect of adjustment to a revolutionary change in technology. Additions and improvements call for supplementary knowledge; major innovations call for the substitution of existing knowledge with new knowledge.

When computers were introduced commercially in the mid-1950s, the emphasis was on engineering and mathematical computations. Generally, the computer was regarded as an automatic high speed calculator, with a memory facility. From the standpoint of education and skill, the significance of it was not in what it could do, or in what it was generally thought it could do, but rather in the new technological, conceptual and operational principles that it introduced. An innovation was introduced which constituted a significant departure from existing technology; a new language was being introduced; and a set of new operational principles was being suggested.

During the early phases of the innovation, perhaps in the first decade of its implementation, the implications for education and skills were very significant: a new set of technical knowledge had to be mastered; there were new concepts; and a new set of operational knowledge had to be grasped. The new knowledge caused the emergence of new occupations and changes in employment classifications. But, the nature of the new technology and the concomitant new knowledge was such that required specialisation on the part of those only who were directly involved with it – the electronics engineers, technicians and programmers. The new knowledge required of those who used the new technology routinely was not of a very high level. Hence for many work activities related to the use of computers, the general levels of education required had not changed to any significant extent.

Subsequent to the initial phase of its introduction, computer technology found application in a wide range of additional activities. But, the new applications, although revolutionary in nature, were mere extensions of the fundamental principles incorporated into the initial theory and technology. It became evident, for example, that in addition to its *Computational potential* – the ability to make programmed decisions, to examine multiple cases, make selections and optimise – *it had memory* – the ability to receive information, store it in memory banks, and provide it to users upon request – and *graphic potential* – the ability to provide the information in a variety of configurations, such as tables, charts, drawings and lines.[11] None of these called for any significant additions to the knowledge of those involved with the operation and use of computers and computer-related instruments and processes.

The technological revolution initiated by electronic instruments and processes is over; and the revolutionary impact on the knowledge and skills of those involved in their operation and use is over, too. Additions to the art and science of the technology, modifications to instruments and processes, and extensions in application to activities and processes will not have the impact it has had in the first decade of application. It is no longer revolutionary in nature, language, performance or role in production processes, whether the production processes involve information on book stocks of libraries, bank accounts, welding of automobile frames, or keeping track of the movement of thousands of railway cars. From now on the revolutionary impact will be on the people at large, not on those involved with the operation and direct use of the technology.

Implications for People at Large

To-date, the technology has been used largely in the performance of specific operational activities within individual enterprises. The impact on the people at large has been largely limited to transactive relationships with enterprises using the technology, such as billing. For the most part people are not aware of the extent to which the technology has become an intermediary between themselves and the enterprises with which they have dealings. The fact that traffic lights are directed by computers does not impact on them, since they did not know who or how traffic lights were operated before the introduction of computer controls. The fact that the school records of the children are now in the computers and different items can be accessed by authorised personnel on request is significant to the school administration, but hardly affects the parents, except perhaps the question of who has access to the information. And the fact that the bank account is now in the computer rather than written on a card, and that when using the Automatic Teller

Machine the communication is with the computer rather than with a teller standing behind a counter, is hardly the sort of revolutionary stuff that would cause problems. The revolutionary impact is yet to come. It will come when the integrated computer–communications systems of individual enterprises become linked together into telematic networks, and when the integrated computer–television–telephone systems of individual households become linked to the network. At that time, the computers of enterprises and households will enter into interactive communication, and thereby revolutionise the work activities in which people engage, and the organisation of work. The nature of the change is difficult to predict precisely. With personal and household computers as surrogates, people will probably work flexible hours, and carry on a more carefree way of life than heretofore. But, the computers may not be put into the role of surrogates; they may instead be put into the role of overseers. The outcome will depend on how the microelectronic infrastructure is organised, and how the people interface with the microelectronic system. The factory system was organised in a way that made most factories prisons, and the workers slaves.[12] It did not have to be that way; the machines did not dictate it. It was organised that way. The organisation of microelectronic work processes could well make us all slaves: computers can be organised to carry out continuous surveillances, to record and monitor every aspect of activity by everyone, and to demand rigid observance of rules and regulations. But, computers do not organise processes and do not themselves command or demand. Whatever they demand and command, they are instructed to do so. Therefore, the nature of relationships that will emerge between microelectronic processes and the people will depend on the organisation and control of the microelectronic infrastructure.

3 The Nature of Microelectronic Technology

Introduction

Three revolutionary technological developments are taking place simultaneously:

1 *Automatic production* – computers, numerically-controlled machines and robots are being integrated into automated production systems – Computer-Aided Design (CAD)/Computer Aided Manufacturing (CAM) Systems.
2 *Videonic communication* – transmission of information from video display terminals to video display terminals via computers – two-way communication without writing on paper, and without the use of voice and speech.
3 *Artificial intelligence* – the implantation of programmes into silicone (and very soon into gallium arsenide) chips, which, in turn, are implanted into machines, instruments, and durables, and thereby transform these into 'intelligent' participants in production processes.

These are, of course, inter-related technologies: videonic communication is critical to automated processes, particularly in the convergence of computer-aided design and computer-aided manufacturing; whereas artificial intelligence, implanted in individual machines and instruments enables them to perform independently of the system, which ensures flexibility in operations. This avoids systemwide shutdowns when individual system parts malfunction, which is a necessary condition for operational efficiency.

The Present Phase

The widespread publicity given to these technologies has created a general impression that their application has become widespread. In fact, in the context of the total production infrastructure in the economy and society, their application is infinitesimal. Even after thirty years of application, all three technologies are still in the very early phases of application. Most production is still mechanical and electromechanical; and most information is still transmitted on paper and by telephone. Automatic production is struggling with marriage problems between often incompatible mechanical technology and electronic parts, instruments and processes; and two-way videonic communication is in its infancy in application, even though the technology appears to have reached maturity. The catalyst in widespread application of electronic technology will be the microprocessor: the capacity to implant microchips into virtually anything presents a potential with revolutionary implications for production processes and society at large. What will go into microchips, where they will be implanted, and for what purposes are issues of cardinal importance to society.

Evolution of the Electronic System

The electronic revolution started with consumer electronics, in the form of transistor radios, calculators, cassettes and video tape recorders. The widespread, worldwide, use of these products created intense demand for electronic chips, which, in turn, became the technical basis for new electronic products, such as watches, cameras, and electronic games. The second phase of the revolution came with the introduction of computers, initially in data-processing, then in information storage and retrieval, followed by computer-aided design processes, and in more recent times increasingly in information transfer functions. It is no longer possible to separate data processing from information processing and transmission. Terms, such as 'telematics', 'computations', 'convergence' are nothing more than attempts to capsulise the essence of multimodal electronic links in production processes – the integration of computers and computer-related instruments, television, telephone and mechanical instruments into automated production systems.

But, integration is some way off; perhaps twenty or more years off. In the meantime, further technical improvements will be introduced to existing equipment – to computers, microprocessors, word processors, reprographic equipment, computer-aided design systems – some new equipment will probably be produced, particularly in the area of communications, and greater effort will probably be put towards improvements in the operation of existing equipment and processes, which involves the design and production of software. To-date, most attention has been focused on the development of hardware, despite the fact that computer technology is almost totally dependent on the nature and quality of the software for operational efficiency.[1] Equipment which performs on programmed instructions will only perform if instructed, and will perform those activities only which it is instructed to perform. The instructions must be precise, and they must be in a language the computer understands.[2] Otherwise, it will remain silent and inoperative.

The Hardware–Software Problem

The lag in software development is responsible for considerable, probably no less than 50 per cent, underutilisation and misutilisation of computers and computer-related processes. Operational inefficiencies often attributed to 'computer failure' are seldom the result of technical malfunctions. Most often they are the result of inappropriate or defective instructions.

This problem has its origin in a traditional engineering perspective. Designers and producers of mechanical and electromechanical equipment have traditionally taken the position that their role was to develop and produce new equipment. The services needed for the operation of the equipment, such as manpower services, for example, were the responsibility of users. If the equipment became under-utilised or utilised inefficiently because of inadequately prepared labour, the responsibility lay with those responsible for the preparation of labour. Designers and producers of computers have taken roughly the same position: the software, they have said, are specific to the requirements of individual computer users. Therefore, it is the responsibility of each user to commission the preparation of software appropriate to the functions to be performed. If computers and computer processes have been underused or misused, the fault is not with the design and quality of the equipment; it is with the design and quality of the software that are being used.

The analogy with labour is substantially correct, and illustrates a problem with which we have had historical experience: like the education and training of labour, the production of software is a slow, labour intensive, process; and like the education and training of labour there is a lag in the production of software, which is often extended by inadequate communication between designers and producers of hardware and designers and producers of software.

The question is whether it is technologically imperative that a traditional relationship between the design and production of machinery and the education and training of labour be maintained in relation to the design and production of computers and the design and production of software needed for their operation. The separation of the two processes will likely create the same kinds of inefficiencies in the operation of microelectronic systems, as the separation of the training of labour from the production and operation of mechanical and electromechanical equipment created over the years. Operational inefficiencies have now become serious enough to cause potential buyers of computer equipment to consider the development of software appropriate to their needs first, and then search for the compatible computer. It has become more difficult to find compatible software, than to find compatible computers.

The time is long past for greater attention to the design and production of software. Traditional thinking about the relationships between the design and production of hardware, and the design and production of the direct services required for the efficient operation of the hardware, based on mechanical and electromechanical processes, must give way to the reality of the abstract requirements of electronic technology. A computer system is constituted of three integral parts: the mechanical part, which is constituted of the moving parts; the electronic parts, which are the processing parts; and the intellectual part, which tells the system what to do. The first and second can be produced in processes enjoying economies of scale; the third is labour intensive, much of it at a high level of intellectual intensity. The manpower required for this third part is generally scarce; which makes it responsible in part for the lag in the development of software, and which explains why hardware producers disassociated the production of hardware from the production of software. They did not wish to be held back by the slow process of software production. But, by not slowing down in the production of hardware that required sophisticated software for efficient operation, they inflicted significant costs on users of hardware in the form of inefficient utilisations and frequent interruptions in operations. As a result, the focus has now shifted from hardware to software. It is estimated that software now accounts for about 85 per cent of computer costs.[3]

The mass production of microprocessors, the production of standard programmes, and ultimately verbal communication with computers will alleviate the problem somewhat. But, like the production of highly specialised manpower, the production of specialised software will remain a slow and laborious process. Therefore, if microelectronisation is to proceed with the minimum of impediments, and if the technological infrastructure is to operate at optimum efficiency, increasing numbers of work functions will have to be standardised, and production processes operated by mass-produced packaged software.

The current phase in the development and application of microelectronic technology can still be characterised as the *innovative* phase: both the technology and its application (software) are at a stage of significant modifications. Equipment and processes are still at the experimental stage, and efforts are being made at innovation of complementary instruments and processes designed to improve the performance of process-systems. There is a proliferation of new equipment, each performing a standard major function plus something else. It is that 'something else' that distinguishes each from its competitors, and it is that something else that is emphasised in its marketing.

Such proliferation in equipment is common in the history of major innovations. But, equally common is the gradual standardisation of equipment over time, and the eventual recognition of what the innovation can do, what functions it can perform, what complementary equipment is necessary for effective and efficient performance, what supportive manpower complement is required, and what it cannot do efficiently. When that phase in the development of the technology is reached, which is the *mature* phase, the proliferation will end, and the 'variations on the basic theme' will be narrowed down.[4]

It is somewhat uncertain at this phase of development to pronounce on whether the narrowing down in processes will be greater or lesser than the narrowing down that has been recorded in mechanical instruments and processes. The evolution of the computer and its ancillary technologies and services certainly indicates changes to-date no fewer than the changes recorded in the history of the automobile, for example, during the early phases of its development, and the proliferation of technologies and services ancillary and related to its production, distribution and use. The only substantive difference between the two is in the level of initial technology: the computer and its ancillary technologies have been initiated at a considerably higher level of technological sophistication than the automobile. Even though the general level of technical knowledge is significantly higher today than it was when the automobile was introduced, the average individual cannot understand, operate, and provide minimal maintenance services to computers and their ancillary technologies. The early models of automobiles were not as removed from the technical competence of the average individual, even though the general level of that competence was considerably lower than it is today.

We are perhaps moving in opposite directions in the development of mechanical and electronic technologies. Mechanical technologies generally were introduced initially at relatively simple levels of technical sophistication, and became complex over time, with the advance in scientific and technical knowledge. In relation to the average individual, this 'progress' in technology meant a movement from the comprehensible to the incomprehensible. By contrast, electronic technologies are being introduced at relatively high levels of technical sophistication, with indications that over time they will become simpler to operate, monitor, and maintain. The average individual may not be able to understand the science and technology involved, but with built-in sensory devices and self-monitoring systems, automatic testing, diagnosis, fault-location and modular replacement, servicing, operation, monitoring, and maintenance can be reduced to the level of changing a light bulb.

Another indication of consequence, with important implications for operational efficiency, is a higher degree of interdependence in the parts of electronic processes than has been the experience with most mechanical processes. Although the introduction of microprocessors will provide system peripherals and key sectors of electronic systems with independent intelligence, such intelligence will be for limited purposes only. The nature and efficiency of electronic systems, at least as conceived currently, centres on the pivotal role of the main computer. The main computer is the heart of the system; if it fails, parts of the system may continue to function briefly and in a limited way, but it will not be long before the system is totally immobilised. The only input in an electromechanical system that would have such a paralysing effect, which is equally important to the electronic system is the flow of power supply.

An outstanding question of consequence is whether electronic systems can be made sufficiently foolproof to minimise the potential for systemwide paralysis. The frequent interruptions, delays, and premature terminations of space flights, of both manned and unmanned craft, indicates that the most sophisticated electronic technology in use today is still some distance away from being operationally foolproof. But, this does not mean it cannot be made so. The history of technological change tells that whenever a technology, or for that matter any factor or process input, became a constraint to operational efficiency, it was eventually removed by corrective technology. We have learned that with technology the question is not one of whether, but how soon.

Most Technology Is Predominantly Mechanical

The technology in use today in advanced industrial economies is still predominantly electromechanical – more than forty years after the introduction of electronics in commercial processes. In manufacturing, construction, transportation (including automobiles), distribution, and offices generally, most of the production functions that are performed by capital instruments are performed by electromechanical instruments. Electronic technology has been making inroads in all processes, but in the context of the total production infrastructure it is still relatively limited. Most welders weld the way they have welded, most secretaries and typists perform their functions the way they performed them, teachers teach in the ways they have taught, nurses nurse in the ways they have nursed, and machinists, mechanics, assembly workers, painters, plumbers, carpenters, sales workers continue to perform the functions they have performed. All of them have had to learn some new functions because of changes in materials, changes in knowledge, and changes in instruments, and all of them had to abandon some of the functions they performed, but such adjustments are a reality of change, not of electronic technology alone.

For the most part, electronic instruments and processes have concentrated into a relatively limited range of activities that are largely labour intensive and specialised: accounting and finance, scientific and engineering activities, research processes, printing, some clerical activities, and telecommunications. The storage and manipulation of data, and the storage and transmission of information are the primary uses to which most microelectronic technology has been put.

The concerns that have been expressed over the past twenty-five years about the implications for work and working, for employment, and for society at large, relate to more widespread uses, which have been expected 'imminently.' But, the time period of the 'imminent' or 'near future' reference is highly speculative when it relates to *the rate* of a new technology, particularly when the new technology, like microelectronics, has the potential for application to a very wide range of activities and processes. Taken by itself, in its technical and scientific potential, the technology may suggest relatively easy application. But, the history of technological change reveals a different reality: the conversion of experimental models into operational systems is fraught with problems; and the more wide-ranging and diverse the activities to which application is intended the greater the technical and operational barriers to application. The world of work is highly heterogeneous in the activities that are being performed, and in the goods and services that are being produced. There are very significant differences between the application of computer technology to data collection, data manipulation and data transmission, and the application of it to the wide-ranging activities performed in an average office. It will be done, but it will take much longer than it took in the application to the limited functions to which the technology has been put to-date. It is conceivable, of course, that many of the work functions currently performed will be eliminated, and many of the remainder will be so standardised as to make their automation relatively easy. But, the process of elimination and standardisation will itself take time. This is why the 'near future' of the 1950s has stretched out into decades and has given the concept 'near' a futuristic time period of 'close distant.' All predictions over the past forty years, about the nature of electronic application, in factories, offices and homes, and on the rate of application have turned out *gross exaggerations*.

In the early phases of the development and application of microelectronic technology, it was generally expected that manufacturing processes were to be the first to experience its impact. The automation scare of the late 1950s was based on such expectations. But, the expectations did not materialise; instead of manufacturing, microelectronics has found the most widespread application to specialised, labour intensive, activities. It is not surprising that this should be so: aside from the fact that the technology is appropriate for many of the work functions performed in labour intensive processes, most of such processes have been relatively limited in the nature of goods and services they could produce.

Capital intensive manufacturing processes did not have such problems. Furthermore, account must be taken of the replacement costs that are involved in factor substitution: the replacement of labour with capital does not involve any replacement costs, except perhaps the training costs sunk into the workers that are to be replaced. By contrast, the replacement of electromechanical equipment with electronic equipment entails replacement of sunk investment capital. Unless the equipment is obsolete or its net cost is recoverable in some way, it becomes a cost consideration in the decision to replace. In other words, under our system of employment contracts, it is less costly to replace people than to replace capital. The replacement cost will influence the rate of introduction of electronic processes.

This reality explains in part why it is more likely to get rapid applications of new technology in capital intensive processes during periods of rapid economic expansion than during periods of stagnation. Aside from the fact that investment capital is more readily available in periods of expansion, such periods are characterised by additions to existing production processes, and the establishment of new processes. Most new technology is usually introduced in conjunction with such additions to processes and new processes. This suggests that in periods of slowdown in economic activity, when there is a decrease in additions to production processes and in the establishment of new processes, the introduction of new technology will slow down. The significantly lower rate of introduction of electronic technology in manufacturing, in commercial establishments, and in offices to-date, than what was predicted ten years ago, can be attributed largely to the slowdown in economic activity over the past decade.

Given economic growth and industrial expansion, the rate of microelectronisation will accelerate. The technology is now available, in a multitude of instruments and processes, and it has passed the test of efficiency and versatility. Wherever it has been applied, even in limited forms relative to its potential – in banking and insurance activities, in offices, and various activities in manufacturing – it has increased output, and made it possible to produce goods and services and perform activities which could not have been done by conventional processes. So, the predictions of the past which have turned out substantially off the mark have been the result not so much of the technology, as of the general state of the economy. This reality should be kept in mind in the assessment of what is being said about future applications: the rate at which manufacturing processes will become increasingly robotised, offices increasingly wired into telematic networks, and homes linked to stores, banks and offices, will depend on the rate of economic expansion. Past experience suggests that two to three years of economic stagnation delays capital renewal by up to ten years. Which means that the technology that was predicted in 1978 to be in place in 1985 will probably be in place in 1995, if the economy recovers by 1984 and maintains a reasonable rate of expansion over the balance of the decade. On the basis of the cyclical behaviour of the economy over the past thirty years, and the rate at which electronic technology has been introduced over the cycle, it would be recklessly optimistic to expect any significant replacement of the existing predominantly electromechanical system with an electronic system – in offices, manufacturing, homes, appliances, cars, etc. – before the year 2030.

Microelectronic Systems in Manufacturing

> The advent of the digital control computer . . . initiated a revolution in the control of industrial plants. The revolution . . . promises to have as profound an impact on technology, economics and society as the industrial revolution had.[5]

Early expectations that entire plant processes will be controlled by one large computer proved unrealistic. Specific process activities became automated, and computers aided in the processing of information and control of certain activities, but the integration of entire processes remained a goal to be achieved.

The advent of the minicomputer and the microprocessor ('computer on a chip') have made attainment of that goal possible: it is now conceptually and technically possible to run an entire industrial process with a chain of interconnected microprocessors, each microprocessor performing the specific tasks appropriate to its position in the process.

The control of complex industrial processes is based upon three concepts:[6] (a) decentralised control, (b) distributed data acquisition, and (c) distributed information processing. A hierarchy of computers, each performing tasks appropriate to its position in the hierarchy, can implement effectively the three concepts.

There is general consensus amongst people knowledgeable in the technology and science of computer systems that advances in computer hardware, computer software and control theory have now made it possible to design control systems which would provide for all functions – actions, interactions and feedbacks – required and expected of complex industrial processes: startup and shutdown procedures, process-control functions, diagnostic programmes, monitoring and response to unexpected developments.

Activities in which varying forms of control have been introduced include:[7]

All kinds of design activities (Computer Aided Design);
Production, material and inventory control;
Numerical control of machine tools and other production equipment;
Automated material handling (robotics);

Automated inspection and testing;
Automated packaging;
Automated warehousing.

A considerable thrust is expected during this and the following decade in the implementation of computer-controlled programmable robots, automatic sensing, group technology concepts, automatic diagnostic/fault-correction systems, automatic tool control and automatic tool changing.[8] In the context of the existing technological infrastructure, the implementation of such innovations suggests revolutionary changes in production processes: they should facilitate the establishment of very large product assembly infrastructures; should improve on the accuracy with which products are produced, and thereby reduce waste and faulty products; should facilitate precision in product reproducibility; should decrease the frequency and length of down-times; and increase efficiency. All of these are positive production signals, which are expected to reduce costs of production.

Various reports indicate that at the end of 1981 about 20 000 robots were employed throughout the world, an estimated 80 per cent of them in Japan. This represents a tenfold increase in their number within five years. And indications are that their employment will accelerate very significantly over the balance of this decade. They are cheaper than human labour; produce a number of times more output than human labour; can do many things that human labour cannot do; they are more reliable than human labour in the performance of the assigned tasks; there is greater consistency in the quality of their work; and, of course, they do not take paid vacations, statutory holidays, and leaves of all kinds, for all kinds of reasons, nor do they go on strike.

At present, most of them are employed in the automobile industry, the aircraft and aircraft parts industry, the steel and aluminium industries, atomic power generating plants, the electrical industry, and major industrial research establishments. They perform precision work, such as drilling, die casting and welding; work that is harmful and dangerous to humans, such as, painting automobiles, and moving radioactive materials; heavy work, such as loading, unloading and stacking materials; machine loading, and a variety of assembly work.

We are in the early phases of a robot invasion of manufacturing. It is held back at present by limited growth in the economy at large and the limited capital investment in manufacturing. But, given a resumption in growth and increase in spending on machinery and equipment, increasing amounts of such spending will be allocated to robots. Most work functions performed by workers in manufacturing are complementary to the work functions performed by the machines they attend and the equipment they use. Most are relatively simple functions, which can be performed by robots more efficiently, with greater precision, and with less waste.

Industrial robots are mechanical workers, equipped with arms and the amount of brain they need for the jobs they are assigned to perform. The work functions to be performed are programmed and deposited in the memory section of the brain. In the course of the work, the arms perform the work functions they are directed to perform, whereas, the brain monitors the work that is being done, retains in memory the work that has been done, and monitors what remains to be done. Like human workers, they are given the job-knowledge they require (programmed) and when the job functions change, they are deprogrammed and reprogrammed in the same way as workers are deskilled and reskilled. The Robot Institute of America defined robots as 'reprogrammable, multi-functional manipulators'.

Whether the invader will be welcomed or resisted will depend on the rate of economic growth and the general level of employment. It will be welcomed as a liberator from the tyranny of machines, the monotony and drudgery of assembly line work and heavy, dangerous and dirty work, if employment generally is increasing; it will be resisted under conditions of generally excessive unemployment.

Even though still relatively limited in its application to manufacturing, microelectronic technology has had considerable impact on both manufactured products and manufacturing processes: it impacted on products through the replacement of mechanical and electromechanical parts with electronic parts, and it impacted on processes through the introduction of programmed controls. In electronic telex machines, one microprocessor replaced 936 moving mechanical parts; in electronic sewing machines, one microprocessor replaced 350 mechanical parts; and in the manufacture of watches, over 1000 assembly operations were reduced to five component parts. These replacements of large numbers of mechanical parts and related assembly operations with one or a few electronic parts have very significant implications for production processes, the rate of production, and the repair and maintenance of manufactured products generally. There are a sufficient number of examples now, in automobile production, electronic calculators, cash registers, and other, to provide a reasonably clear indication of future trends. Increasingly, new models of durable goods will contain fewer and fewer mechanical parts.

There is evidence that the microelectronisation of certain manufactured products and manufacturing processes has resulted in significant productivity gains.[9] The labour time involved in the production of some products has fallen by as much as 95 per cent. Yet, questions have been raised about the direction and focus of some microelectronisations. Applications do not appear to be directed to activities that are critical to the cost and efficiency of industrial processes. For example, it is estimated that 60 per cent to 70 per cent of the cost of manufacturing is in planning, scheduling and control of equipment, and only 30 per cent to 40 per cent of the cost is in the physical making of a part or product. Similarly, it is reported that in standard manufacturing processes a part spends 5 per cent of the time being machined, and the other 95 per cent of the time moving and waiting to be used.[10] Yet, the focus has been on the physical making of the product – on the 30–40 per cent of the cost, not on the 60–70 per cent. One of the principal theoreticians on CAD/CAM technology commented: 'Some plants have more expeditors than people making things.'[11] This suggests that in the development and application of microelectronic technology to manufacturing, efficiency considerations were not given the relative weight that was warranted. The emphasis in recent years to computer-aided design technology and its application to planning, scheduling and equipment control seems more in line with the costs and critical activities in production processes. But, then, such developments are not uncharacteristic of the application of a major technological change. The pervasiveness of microelectronic technology dictates widespread experiments in application. It is inevitable that in the period of experimentation applications will be tried into all kinds of activities and processes.

Microelectronics and Communications

A distinctive and revolutionary development in electronic communication is *communication without writing on paper and without voice and speech*. It is *communication via the video-screen*.

In ages past communication was largely limited to voice communication (face to face and then by telephone) and by writing (hand writing and then typewriting). The advent of film, television and the computer added to the modes of communication, but speech and writing remained the essential means of communication. The video display terminal, with keyboard and two-way communication, is making it possible to communicate without writing on paper and without the use of voice and speech. All requests for information, which is the essence of communication, can be made electronically, and all responses can be provided electronically. In time we will become accustomed to the use of the *videobox* as a perfect substitute for the *voicebox* and the written message for most exchanges of information.

The cumbersome and imperfect system of communication in practice at present – writing on paper and its physical delivery, face to face transmission of information, and transmission of information by telephone – will gradually become limited to social activity. In the search of information about goods and services – their availability, varieties, prices, locations, terms, etc – it will become easier to obtain on the video screen, examine in detail and at leisure, than through telephone, newspaper, or personal visits to different places. Furthermore, we will gradually recognise the fact that voice communication tends to influence decisions, whereas script communication via the video screen is more neutral in influence. Therefore, decisions are likely to become more rational when based on information obtained from the video screen.

The system of communication in effect at present is largely one of *graphonics* (*grapho* for writing, and *phonics* for voice and speech). Computers and telecommunications technology are ushering a system of *videonics* – visual communication by means of video display terminals. Writing on paper by hand or typewriter will be progressively replaced by the keyboard attached to the video display terminal, whereas the use of voice and speech will become progressively limited to consultations, discussions and social purposes. In time, speech will become the means of communication with computers, which will eliminate the need for special language of communication with them. Considerable progress has been reported in speech recognition and synthesis by computers. In the not too distant future, perhaps by the end of the 1990s decade, we should be able to give computers verbal instructions and receive in response the requested information, as well as questions and statements.

The change from graphonics to videonics will necessarily be slow, but it is unmistakable: given an integrated computer–telecommunications system in the nature of the telephone system in existence at present, with computers linked to television sets and video display terminals in homes, stores, offices, banks, etc., there would be no conceivable reason to resort to writing by hand or typewriter, or to the telephone for transmission of information. Terminal-to computer-to terminal communication will eliminate two of the serious barriers to efficient transmission of information, namely, the physical delivery of written communications, and direct access (availability) to the party that is being sought at the other end of the telephone line. Much time is being wasted in the delivery of written information, and equally much is being wasted in attempts to get people on the telephone.

The conversion to a *videonic* network will depend on the rate at which households, stores, banks, offices, and other establishments are equipped with computers and video display terminals; the rate at which they are linked together into two-way interactive networks; the rate at which the stock and flow of information is organised so that the system can perform its function of information dissemination effectively; and the rate at which the public at large can be made to use the system effectively and efficiently. The first two of these variables are technical, and no longer present any serious problem. Communications technology has now reached a level of development when a videonic network is an imminent possibility. The other two variables are organisational: the effectiveness of the system depends not on the technical efficiency with which the system provides information, but rather on the nature of information it provides. Which means that the stock of information to which the system has access, the flow of current information, and the update of the stock of information are critical to the effectiveness and use of the system.

The basic communications network for a videonic system is largely in place: the telephone is in widespread use, and the television cable system is well established. The computer and computer-related hardware instruments are becoming widely available at prices that make them increasingly accessible to the population at large; and a number of two-way communication systems are being tested. As to public acceptance of a system which will require less and less speech communication as a means of information transmission, the increasing use of automatic bank machines for deposits, withdrawals, the transfer of funds and payments of bills, where all communication is via keyboard and video display indicates public acceptance. Indeed, as more and more of the transmission of information is carried out by means of keyboard and video displays, people will find speech communication an increasingly inefficient and cumbersome means of information transmission.

Does the establishment of a *videonic* system mean the on-set of the paperless office? 'The vision of the paperless office' wrote *The Economist* 'is future-gazing nonsense.'[12] Yet, conceptually it is quite possible to visualise a paperless office system. The office is largely an information processing centre; and paper is used to communicate information, to store information, and to inbed information on it for reference purposes. All these can be done electronically. Information deposited in computers can be accessed, examined and communicated via the electronic system to anyone who is linked to it; it can be deposited in the computer for storage and reference; and all kinds of non-paper recording devices can be used to record things for quick reference.

One of the main reasons that the paperless office is slow to develop is the absence of an electronic system like the telephone system to link electronic offices together. Unless an electronically integrated office can communicate with other offices electronically, it will have to keep in place the conventional paper and telephone system for external communication. This reduces significantly the advantages of electronic communication. But, there is no doubt that when an electronic system becomes established, and industrial, commercial and institutional enterprises become equipped with computers, computer-related instruments and video display terminals, the way they are now equipped with telephones and television cables, a *videonic* system will come into being. There would be no conceivable reason then for the use of paper. When the office can dispatch and receive via the VDT any information, to anywhere, from anywhere, at any time, there would be no reason to put it on paper.

The existing paper-based system of information processing and communication is very costly at the management level of operations. Contrary to common belief, office costs are not mostly secretarial and clerical costs, and inefficiencies in office operations are not rooted in clerical and secretarial processes. They will be found largely in management activities. One estimate put 75 per cent of office costs to management activities, and only 12 per cent to secretarial services.[13] This suggests a misplaced emphasis in the electronisation of office activities: instead of electronising clerical and secretarial functions, emphasis should perhaps have been put to the electronisation of some management functions. The typical manager spends 50 per cent of the time producing, reading, editing, and discussing reports. Writing by hand on paper, editing and re-writing are very slow processes. If some of these activities were to be electronised and sped-up time will be vacated for more important activities, such as contemplatation, planning, consultation and decision-making. It is possible to visualise the manager of the future organising reports, memos, letters, documents, or whatever, on the VDT, depositing them in the memory bank at the end of the day to be recalled the next day, or on the home VDT in the evening for further examination, instructing subordinates to access them and provide their inputs; and upon the completion of them to instruct the computer to communicate them to all who should have access to them. Clearly, this will require a significant change in the manager's attitude towards work functions, since such an activity will involve functions associated with secretaries and typists. But, there is no such attitude problem with young managers, brought-up in the computer age. They are accustomed to turn around on their swivel chairs and operate the keyboard on their office computer-word processor. Nevertheless, for the present, and the near future (the time that it takes for present management to be replaced) the association of typing with secretaries remains an obstacle, and in addition, many managers cannot type and probably will refuse to learn. If the manager cannot type, most of the potential productivity is lost. This obstacle will be removed with the introduction of desk-top terminals which can be inputed by voice, but these are a distant future possibility.

The ultimate office system and the system of communication generally will be the videonic system. At present we are still labouring under the cumbersome *graphonic* system. The advent of the video display terminal is introducing a system of *videophonics*, which eliminates writing and relies on visual and vocal communication. The trend towards videonics is unmistakable, as witnessed by the very limited vocal communication amongst those who are linked together via video display terminals.

4 Stimulants and Barriers

An examination of microelectronic processes in place throughout the economy will establish that computers and other electronic applications to production processes, are still a very small part of the total production infrastructure of the economy. In view of the many positive characteristics that electronic instruments and processes contain why has the rate of application been so slow? On the other hand, is it conceivable that the technology is so deceptive that we fail to notice its creeping intrusion into every-day activity? Children are using a variety of electronic instruments and processes in education and play; the operation of our cars is increasingly regulated by electronic instruments; we are being watched electronically in banks, department stores, airports and thousands of other places; our names, addresses, occupations and financial standing are stored, retrieved, and transmitted electronically from country to country; and we carry electronic watches, cook in electronically regulated stoves and microwave ovens, heat our homes with gas, oil or electricity whose flows are regulated electronically, watch television and listen to radio, both of which are largely electronic instruments performing a service function produced almost entirely electronically.

What do we mean then when we say the application of electronics has been slow? It is that major electronic processes and interactive systems which were expected to be in place ten or more years ago are yet to become operational. Electronic Funds Transfer Systems (EFTS), Automatic Checking Out (OCA), Point of Sale Systems (POS), Automatic Teller Machines (ATM), Computer Aided Design (CAD), and Computer Aided Manufacturing (CAM) systems are still at the experimental phase of development. Some ATMs have been installed, and some CAD and CAM systems are operational, but they are limited in both numbers and range of operations.[1]

It is too early in the age of microelectronics to delve into the question of why does it take so long to introduce technological systems which have been reported long ago ready for introduction. There can be all sorts of problems, some technical and some operational. When the same question is asked in relation to the industrial revolution, an examination of the record will show that delays were caused by lack of some materials, the failure of some invention, faults in prototype equipment, lack of skills, resistance to change, inadequate investment capital, work organisation problems, distribution problems, repair and maintenance problems, security problems, and many other. In every sector of the economy there was some obstacle, some barrier to be removed before progress could be made: in agriculture, the problem was common rights and the lack of winter fodder; in mining, the problem was flood water and how to deal with it efficiently; in the metal trades, shortage of materials was the problem; and in textiles, inadequate supply of yarn. In addition, transportation presented problems, and trade and credit were controlled by monopolies, which for reasons of control limited the rate of economic expansion.[2] Slow economic expansion inevitably slows the rate of technological change, since it bears on the need for technological replacement and on the capacity to invest in new technology.

Delays in Microelectronisation

A plethora of explanations exist for the slower rate of microelectronic systems development than the rate that was projected ten or more years ago. But, three developments seem to have been primarily responsible: equipment incompatibility, delays in software development, and scarcity of qualified manpower.

The problems with equipment are not unlike the problems that were encountered in the early phases of application of mechanical technology – incompatibility amongst different units of the new technology and the existing technology. Most electronic systems consist of three technical elements: the electronic circuitry; the mechanical parts; and the software system. Operational efficiency on the technical side depends on the successful marriage of electronics and mechanics, and on the development of appropriate software for each operational system.

The marriage has been much more difficult than anticipated: since electronic processes have traditionally been developed largely independently from mechanical processes, problems have arisen with the integration of the two; and since software development has been separate from hardware development, widespread problems have been encountered with incompatibility of hardware and software. In addition, incompatible electrical and mechanical parts have plagued system operations; and the development of software for complex operations have proven more difficult than anticipated.

As a result, the development of microelectronic *systems* has slowed down markedly in recent years. The emphasis is once again on the individual units – the personal micro-computer, the word processor, the robot – and not so much on the linking together of all sorts of units into integrated production systems.

A fundamental principle in automation is that optimum performance cannot be achieved until the system is complete. Therefore, to the extent that various considerations make it necessary that the system be introduced on a piecemeal basis, care must be taken to ensure that the automated phases (parts) are compatible with one another, and that ultimately all automated parts can be linked together into one integrated system. Incompatible parts hinder integration, and involve considerable replacement costs.

Incompatibility in automated equipment appears to be more widespread than is commonly thought, and appears to be responsible in part for the slower progress in integration than the available technology would dictate. Failure at comprehensive technology planning by industry, increasing competition amongst producers and distributors of automated equipment, and the acceleration in application of innovations to automated equipment, all have contributed to considerable incompatibility in parts of automated processes within individual establishments. But *the main problem appears to be the approach taken towards the introduction of automated processes*: the approach is from the parts rather than from the system. Furthermore, not only are the parts introduced on a piecemeal basis, but oftentimes they are introduced without any apparent attempt to understand where or how they might fit into an integrated system.

An example of this is provided by the introduction of word processors. There is no evidence that their selection and introduction is being done with consideration of the nature of an integrated office system in which they will be an operational part. Generally, they are regarded as units in themselves; and the decisions to invest in them are taken in isolation of the total system of which they are a part. Yet, their optimum performance, from the standpoint of their technological capacity, cannot be achieved until they are linked with other automated parts into an integrated office communications network.

Technical problems have not been the only problems in the utilisation of the new equipment and processes. Equally serious have been the *operational problems*. There are significant differences between the technical capacity of a system and the capacity of an organisation to utilise the technical capacity: management must generate work for the system; there must exist an appropriate mix of manpower for the operation of the system; and management must have the capacity to use the output of the system efficiently and effectively. Many electronic systems have proven to be too fast for business and institutional bureaucrats accustomed to ponderous decision-making. Indeed, some of the systems are decades ahead of the capacities of senior management to use them effectively; much of the information produced for them is not used at all! The Senior Vice-President of a Bank confided that 80 per cent of the computer information placed on his desk each morning was of no use to him. He viewed it as information 'churned out automatically every day because the computer was programmed to churn it out'. This indicated that the organisation of work functions and employment responsibilities has yet to respond to the requirements of the electronic system. It will probably take another two decades before the executive suite is occupied by people who will use the system effectively. Until then operational constraints will continue to emanate from the executive suite, and the rate of application will continue to be slower than it is technically possible.

Another well-known impediment to which frequent reference is made is the *scarcity of qualified manpower*. Computer-related manpower has been generally scarce, both on the technical side and the operational side, and there has been critical scarcity of high level software specialists. This has been a serious problem, and will continue to be a problem, particularly for complex system operations. The kinds of people that can undergo education and training for high-level software development are scarce, and the work involved in the development of high level software requires a degree of intensity that cannot be carried out for very long periods of time. Therefore, unless the technology is so changed as to incorporate or eliminate the need for some of the complex and interrelated functions, a perpetual manpower scarcity will remain, which will impose a long term constraint on the rate of implementation and utilisation of electronic systems.

Other factors to which references have been made for the slow rate in systems development have been a lack of awareness of the technology, particularly in relation to specific applications; the relatively high costs, particularly software costs; difficulties in estimating operating costs, and the return to potential investment capital; uncertainties about service and maintenance of equipment, re-inforced by reports of costly downtimes; inadequate understanding of what microelectronic processes can do; conservative attitudes of some managers; workforce resistance; and industrial relations issues.[3]

Work Organisation as a Barrier

Changes in technology effect the ways in which people work, the ways in which work is organised, the work relationships amongst processes within individual systems, and inter-occupational relationships. It is not unusual then to expect radical changes in functional relationships at work places as a result of the introduction of microelectronic systems. Jobs change, work functions within jobs change, relationships amongst jobs change, people have to learn new ways of doing things, and means of communication change, which affect relationships amongst people and between people and institutions.

Whether such effects become barriers to microelectronisation depends on how effectively individuals, organisations, and society at large accommodate the change. It is inevitable that some people will be concerned about losing their jobs, and respond negatively towards the change; some will resist it because it dictates changes in management style; some will approach the change cautiously because of uncertainties and potential problems; some of the successful practitioners in trades and professions will resist it because they themselves do not see it as necessary for their own efficiency, and may even regard it as a threat to their efficiency; some may resist it because it will effect occupational boundary lines and dilute the work functions of their occupations; and some will resist it because of concerns that they will not be able to cope with the resultant changes in work responsibilities.

Concerns of this nature dictate a gradual approach to microelectronisation, particularly in processes which will continue to employ human labour. Where human intervention is eliminated, the problem becomes one of finding alternative employments for displaced workers; where human involvement continues to be needed, but work activities are altered radically and inter-occupational relationships are changed, the problem becomes one of human adjustment to a new work environment, new work functions, and new work relationships. From the standpoint of the introduction and efficient utilisation of new technology, displacement of labour may be less of an obstacle than adjustment of employees to radically altered work environments.

Barriers to the Introduction of Office Technology

Notwithstanding the very considerable publicity given to on-going and pending office automation, the penetration of microelectronic and telecommunications technology in offices is still relatively low.

A number of economic, institutional and social factors are acting to slow the rate of penetration:

(1) The high costs of switching to electronic office systems. Despite price declines, a switch to microelectronic/telecommunications based office technology is expensive, compared to traditional office equipment. While a word processor can be purchased for $10 000 to $20 000 depending upon the software, a conventional electric typewriter can be purchased for $1000. Computer facilities, facsimile machines, intelligent copiers and other microelectronic based equipment increase the costs even further. Furthermore, the cost of equipment is only part of the total capital outlay: the cost of installation, the cost of linking devices, the cost of running parallel manual systems while the inevitable 'bugs' are worked out of the electronic system, and the total costs of switching to electronic technology, add substantially to conversion costs.

Thus, even though much has been written about the declining cost of microelectronic office technology, a substantial initial capital outlay is required to switch from electromechanical processes to individual units of electronic equipment, and ultimately to the fully integrated electronic office system. In a sector where investment per worker has traditionally been low, it becomes especially difficult to justify a switch to technology which is expensive relative to the current office technology, and essentially unproven in actual office environments.

(2) The diversity of office activities. Most office activities are ill-defined, cannot be standardised, and are not amenable to traditional data processing approaches. In the past, the automation of office activities worked best when applied to high volume, repetitive, standardised activities such as inventory control, accounts payable, accounts receivable and invoicing. Although ultimately increasing numbers of work functions will be either automated or eliminated, efforts to-date have not been crowned with the anticipated success. The large number of diverse office activities require complicated software, which have proven difficult to write.

(3) The continuing shortage of software specialists remains a serious barrier. In addition, the writing of software for the multitude of office activities has proven considerably more difficult than anticipated. Sophisticated hardware do not make an effective office communications system: the critical element is the software. Reference was

made above to the fact that unlike the manually operated mechanical technology of the distant past, and unlike the electrically operated and labour attended mechanical technology currently in use, electronic technology has to be instructed to perform. The language of instruction is very difficult, and the more complex the process the more difficult it becomes. Communication is a very complex process. There is general consensus that the software will hold back the rate of implementation and the rate of efficient utilisation of electronic systems.

(4) Shortages of systems analysts are often mentioned as a delaying factor, but there is some uncertainty on whether the problem is shortage or misutilisation. There is some evidence that continuing developmental problems with the science and technology of microelectronic processes may be responsible for the shortages. When a resource is misutilised because of technical and organisational inefficiencies, the resultant shortages are not related to supply. They are related rather to the inefficiencies of production processes. In such cases, the corrective measures should focus on the efficiency of utilisation, not on the supply.

(5) The resistance of office workers. Computer-based office technology can potentially have a large impact on the way the office is organised, on the work functions performed, on the flow of information in the office, and on the overall office environment. Fears, uncertainties and a reluctance to move away from familiar organisational structures and work methods, generate resistance to the technology at all levels of employment. Furthermore, inadequate knowledge about the technology, reinforced by rumour of mass displacement create apprehension, which manifests itself in uncertain and cautious approaches to the utilisation of electronic equipment. The prospect of direct interaction with the machines is found demeaning, and the disruption of familiar work methods, work flows and functional relationships, rather disturbing. The integrated electronic office is not a mere piece of equipment to be installed in an office, nor is it just a computer which has significant implications for the work process, but effects directly only a few. It is a system of communication, with implications for the entire organisational structure, introducing entirely different methods of communication than those to which people have been accustomed: people want to verbalise, face to face or over the telephone, they want to visit, to ask questions and to get answers from people not from inanimate objects; and people want to

be in contact with other people in the work process. Even where only partial integration has been introduced, the work environment has become eerie – a graveyard of silence: telephones do not ring, people do not talk, typewriters do not clang. The silence is so intense and overpowering, the unaccustomed tend to either want to scream or to whisper.

(6) The continuing uncertainty about the legal status, security and privacy of information stored and transmitted by electronic systems is another problem. As long as the uncertainty remains, applications will be limited to in-house operations, which means that the communications capabilities of electronic systems will find limited use.

(7) Limited evidence of increase in *overall* office productivity. One of the major problems in discussing the effects of office automation is to separate the potential effects of the technology itself from the effects of the technology in actual applications. The literature on the 'automated office' focuses almost exclusively on the potential of the technology itself. But, while the technological potential to implement electronic office systems is a necessary condition for the achievement of greater efficiency in the handling of information flows, it is not a sufficient condition to ensure that efficiencies will be achieved in real world applications. In many instances, gaps exist between the technological potential of the system, and the actual productivity increases experienced in working office settings.

(8) The capacity of microelectronic instruments and processes has beeen substantially greater than the volumes of work processed in the average office. Operational efficiency dictates a relationship between the production capacities of instruments and processes, and the actual and planned volume of work to be produced. To the extent that the capacities of instruments and processes exceed substantially the actual and anticipated volumes of work, investment in them will be postponed until such time as either instruments and processes with lower capacities are produced, or the volumes of work increase to higher levels. The production of mini-computers and other micro instruments and processes is a response to this barrier – to make it possible, from the standpoint of cost and effeciency in utilisation, for the smallest office to invest in microelectronic instruments.

Failures in Office Efficiency

There is no evidence to-date that electronic processes have increased *the overall* productivity in office work. Individual electronic instruments and processes have increased the productivity in the areas of activity to which they have been applied, but there is no evidence that such increases have become reflected in the productivity of the total office process. This suggests that the improvements in productivity in areas of activity to which electronic instruments and processes have been applied, have tended to somewhat dissipate through the office system. Such an outcome bears negatively, of course, on decisions to invest in office technology.

Amongst the factors responsible for the failure of office productivity to increase, three have been cited most frequently:

(a) The failure to automate managerial and professional activities. The office is a multifaceted operation: the increase in productivity at one level of its operation does not necessarily mean a general increase in productivity. The secretarial level of operation may increase its output, but that may be offset by inefficiencies at the managerial and professional levels. The electronic equipment installed in offices to-date is largely designed to increase the efficiency in clerical and secretarial work functions. Yet, the sources of inefficiency in those work functions will not be found in the ways and means by which clerks and secretaries perform their work functions. They will be found rather largely with those who provide clerks and secretaries with the work to be done. In most instances a clerk or secretary is not productive because inadequate work has flowed down, or instructions on the nature of work that is required are inadequate or imperfect, causing the work to be re-done, or the writing has been imperfect, requiring numerous revisions, and so on. The question arises then, in what way will the instruments and processes at the clerical and secretarial levels improve office productivity. The secretaries and clerks will perform their work faster. But, unless those who provide secretaries and clerks with work improve their own productivity, the increase in efficiency at the clerical and secretarial levels of work may result in more and longer periods of idleness for clerks and secretaries. There is increasing recognition that productivity in the office will not increase significantly until automation streamlines the functional activities of managerial and professional personnel. Considering that clerical and secretarial functions account for no more than about 20 per cent of office costs, it is not too difficult to waste efficiencies achieved at that level of office operations.

(b) Failure to integrate office technology. An important condition for the integration of office technology is the ability of the different pieces of office equipment to 'speak the same language' or what manufacturers call 'plug-in compatibility'. This condition has often not been met. Intense competition amongst large numbers of vendors has manifested itself in the use of different communications protocols to 'lock out' the competition; the prevailing opinion in industry is that this condition will continue as long as competition remains at the present level. The fully integrated office will await the establishment of common communications standards by the multitude of manufacturers, or the emergence of one or a few manufacturers each of whom will produce all equipment and devices that will constitute the integrated office.

(c) Failure to adjust to the technology. Any technological change involves new knowledge, and dictates adjustments to the ways in which work activities are performed. The effectiveness with which a technological change will be put into operation depends on the rapidity and effectiveness of the adjustment process – the rate at which the new knowledge can be absorbed, old knowledge and work habits discarded, and appropriate adjustments put into effect wherever such are dictated throughout the production, distribution and user system. Failure of any part of the system to respond in accordance with the operational requirements of the technology will mean that the technology will be underused or misused. For example, the unwillingness of an executive officer to use the keyboard of a video display terminal to access information from the computer will contribute significantly to the inefficient use of a computer and communications system. Similarly, the introduction of a word processor in a work setting which has limited editing functions will mean that the word processor will be used largely for typing activities. Such substitution of typewriters would be a very inefficient and costly substitution. And again, if conditions at the secretarial level are appropriate for the efficient use of word processors and other electronic instruments, but management which inputs the secretarial level fails to accommodate the work requirements of the new processes, the system will still be underutilised. Clearly, for an operational system to function efficiently, all parts involved with the system must function efficienctly. Individual parts can be catalysts to system efficiency and they can be bottlenecks to system efficiency. Inefficiencies in the utilisation of new equipment tend to bear down on the rate of application of new equipment. Producers and distributors must show that investment in it does in fact increase productivity.

To summarise: the rate of application has been considerably lower than the projected rate. The 'office of the future' is still in the future. In the meantime, a variety of electronic devices will be installed, some of them dummy peripherals linked to computers and word processors, and some with limited intelligence contained in imbedded micro chips. Individuals knowledgeable of the technology concede that it will take a long time, and very considerable development and operational costs, before integrated systems become operationally efficient. At the present stage of the technology, the computer and the peripheral parts are more efficient individually than as an integrated whole.

Stimulants to Microelectronisation

The factors that stimulate investment in microelectronic instruments and processes are largely the same factors that stimulated investment in mechanical instruments and processes:

1 To perform work activities which cannot be performed by non-electronic instruments and processes;
2 Need to increase the volume and range of goods or services, which cannot be done with an increase in existing capital/labour combinations;
3 Scarcity of qualified manpower;
4 Changes in relative prices of capital and labour;
5 Quest for increase in effiency.

Most activities to which electronic instruments and processes have been applied – in banks, airline establishments, offices, manufacturing processes – attest to (a) the performance of scores of activities which could not have been performed by conventional non-electronic processes; (b) significant increases in the range of activities performed and services produced; and (c) significant increases in production capacity. In addition, all attest to varying degrees of pressure to offset the constraints on expansion imposed by scarcity in qualified workers.

Changes in the relative prices of capital and labour have been an important influence in decisions to invest in microelectronic instruments and processes. Before the introduction of microelectronics, and while the prices of microelectronic instruments were high relative to the price of labour, labour intensive processes found it advantageous to remain labour intensive. Where relative prices favoured the employment of capital, as in manufacturing, transportation, printing and utilities, capital became the predominant factor of production. Thus, capital investment per office worker is estimated to have averaged at only about $2,000, mostly in desks, filing cabinets, calculators, typewriters and copiers, whereas the capital investment per factory worker is estimated at 15–20 times that amount.[4]

In recent years, two developments have shifted the advantage to capital: one is the successive increases in wages and salaries in service employments, most of them considerably in excess of increases in productivity; and the other is the successive decrease in prices of microelectronic instruments, while their capacities and productivities are increasing. When a personal computer can be bought for $1,500, it is difficult to resist investing in it, particularly when the wages of secretarial and clerical personnel are expected to continue increasing.

Efficiency considerations are, of course, paramount in decisions to allocate capital funds to microelectronic instruments. Management must be convinced that the investment will increase efficiency in operations and decrease operating costs. As indicated earlier, herein will be found the reason for the considerably slower rate of microelectronisation of goods-producing processes than of offices and services-producing processes. Most goods-producing processes are capital intensive, and it is difficult to demonstrate that replacement of the mechanical infrastructure with an electronic one will increase productivity to an extent that would justify the investment; whereas offices and services-producing processes have been for the most part labour intensive, with forms of work organisation and work functions that are inherently inefficient. It is not difficult to demonstrate the increase in efficiency from the replacement of a typewriter with a word processor, or from the introduction of a computer in a personnel office or in an accounting office.

Consider the efficiency implications of microelectronic instruments and processes in communication: the work of perhaps 80 per cent of the working population is communication work – verbal face-to-face, verbal over the telephone, radio, and television, reports, letters, memoranda. Most of it is very inefficient, and often very ineffictive. Yet, most communication, whether business or private, is carried out by such means and processes. Inefficient and ineffective communication is a most serious imperfection, and imposes a very heavy cost burden on the economy and society.

In verbal communication, time is wasted in establishing thought communication; time is wasted in establishing verbal communication; and time is wasted in establishing verbal–thought communication. We are distracted by other people's appearance, by their dress, their looks, by the ways they talk, the ways they seat or stand, by their mannerisms. Effective verbal communication requires not only that two persons speak the same language, but also that they establish face to face or telephone contact, and that they both think about the subject on which they communicate. Communication will be ineffective if one of the parties thinks about subjects other than the subject on which they communicate. The all too frequent apology 'Sorry, I was thinking about something else', illustrates the point.

In transactive relationships, when one of the parties in the communication process provides specific services on request, verbal communication is inefficient and burdensome. By programming the party providing the service to respond precisely to questions and requests put to it, much unnecessary communication can be eliminated.

In written communication, time is wasted in slow writing by hand or typewriter; and much time is wasted in delivery and distribution of letters, reports and memoranda. Electronic mail will correct much of that: letters, messages and reports will be deposited in the memory banks of electronic instruments to be accessed by the people to whom they are intended when necessary. No physical delivery, no duplicate copies, no physical distribution.

The application of microelectronic technology in certain service and communication activities, such as banking, travel and offices, facilitated the undertaking of activities and services which could not have been undertaken with non-electronic processes, and provided a degree of efficiency that was not attainable with the largely labour intensive processes of the past. Consider, for example, the difference in efficiency in depositing, withdrawing and transferring funds from one account to another through a teller performing all the tasks manually, and through automatic teller machines. The inefficiency and frequent ineffectiveness of verbal communication is eliminated; the burden, inefficiency and frequent ineffectiveness of hand-written communication is eliminated; and the inefficiencies inherent in human physical activity within a system of work organisation, such as searching for the customer's card-record, completing forms manually, recording transactions, and scores of other manual functions associated with the communication and service processes are eliminated.

A more efficient communication process does not, of course, always result in more efficient communication: efficiency depends on the nature of actions that are initiated, the nature and speed of responsive reactions, the decisions that are made, and the transactions that are completed. In automated processes, the reaction is often instantaneous, and within the programme of instructions that govern the responses of the microelectronic processes, decisions are taken and transactions are completed automatically. In human communication the reaction may be delayed so much as to neutralise the greater efficiency of the microelectronic communication process. This suggests that if microelectronic processes are to increase the efficiency of communication amongst people an element of compulsion will have to be built into the system. The technology must be made to dictate limits to human procrastination.

The Rate of Microelectronisation

To determine the possible rate of microelectronisation in different industry groups and work activities, account must be taken of (a) the rate of economic growth and associated capacity to invest, (b) the state of the art and science of the technology in relation to the various work activities and processes, and (c) the stimulants and barriers examined above.

An attempt has been made to project the rate of diffusion amongst industry groups on the basis of the state of the art and science of the technology.[5] The introduction of Electronic Technology, Computer Technology, and Computer-Aided Design (CAD)/Computer-Aided Manufacturing (CAM) Systems were rated on a scale of 0–10 over a period of 5–10 years beginning in 1980. The ratings were as follows:

Activities in *Agriculture and other primary industries were rated 1 and 2*, except certain metal mining activities which were given 5 for electronic technology and computer technology, and petroleum and natural gas, which were given 6 for electronic technology and 10 for computer technology.

Manufacturing was mostly rated 2–4, except for motor vehicles manufacturing which, very optimistically in my opinion, was rated 10 in all three technologies; aircraft and aircraft parts manufacturing which was rated 10 in electronic technology and computer technology, and 6 in CAD/CAM; iron and steel mills, which were rated 8 in electronic technology, 10 in computer technology and 6 in CAD/CAM; printing, publishing and allied industries, which were also given 8, 10 and 6; radio and television receivers manufacturers, 10, 6 and 8; and a few others.

The Construction industry was rated 2, 5 and 3; Transportation, Storage and Communication 9, 9 and 3; and Electric Power, Gas and Water Utilities 8, 8 and 2.

From the standpoint of employment, the rate at which activities in the service sector are microelectronised is, of course, of critical importance.

Activities in Trade were rated 6 for electronic technology, 8 for computer technology, and 2 for CAD/CAM – Foodstores 6, 6 and 2; department stores 6, 6 and 4; clothing stores 4, 4 and 0; and all other retail establishments 4, 4 and 0 – not the rapid and widespread microelectronisation projected by manufacturers and distributors of electronic equipment and processes.

Finance, insurance and real estate were rated 8, 10 and 0 – a rating that is proving to be very close to reality.

Community and business services were given ratings of 8, 9 and 0; and *Public administration and defence*, a somewhat optimistic 10, 10 and 2.

On the basis of the art and science of the technology, Scrimgeour and his professional associates were probably correct in the industry ratings. Sporadic reports on the rate of microelectronisation in various industries and activities over the past three years suggest that they would have been reasonably close to reality if advanced industrial economies had continued to grow at the rates in effect in 1979–80, when the projections were made. But, since then the capacities of industries, institutions, governments, and enterprises generally to invest in new technology have diminished, and the rate of microelectronisation has slowed down significantly.

The Responses of Unions

History attests to the fact that resistance to technological change in the form of withdrawal of services (railway firemen, elevator constructors, printers) or in the form of job control (apprentice-journeymen ratios, shop arrangements, production–process rules and regulations) has seldom saved any jobs. Such measures have delayed the implementation of some technological changes, and put off temporarily the displacement of some workers, but neither prevented implementation nor avoided displacement.

Unions face two negative choices in relation to technological changes: opposition, which may save jobs in the short-run, but, if successful in holding off the introduction of new technology, will most likely result in the loss of jobs over the long-run; and acquiescence, which may result in some immediate displacements of workers and skills, but gives historical promise of more jobs in the long run.

An examination of the choices that have been made suggests a close relationship between the nature of the choice, the nature of the union organisation, and the quality of the union leadership. *The nature of the union organisation* is important because a union whose membership is constituted of one skill is more likely to oppose technological changes which threaten the destruction of the skill, than one which is constituted of a number of skills. The long-standing conflict between railways and their firemen to the introduction of the diesel locomotive, and between newspapers and their typographers in relation to the introduction of printing automation, are amongst the most recent examples.

The historical record also indicates that the most difficult accommodations have been those which involved long-established skills, and one skill organisations: whenever new technology threatened the continuing existence of a skill, the union organisation faced the dual problems of employment security for its members and its own existence. The negotiation of alternative employments for its members, in the jurisdictions of other unions, or arrangements for severance pay and early retirements, constitute in effect the negotiation of the union's own demise. Few unions elected to do so voluntarily.

Unions facing such a dilemma have commonly insisted that their members be trained to operate the new equipment: the organisations of locomotive firemen have insisted that firemen should continue to be employed on diesel locomotives as assistants to engine drivers, and the International Typotraphical Union has insisted that its members continue to be employed in capacities related to the operation of the computerised equipment.

The attitudes manifested in such demands have a historical precedent. During the industrial revolution craft unions took the stand that the machines that were being introduced into craft shops were to be operated by craftsmen, even if their craft skills were not required for the operation. The conflict between The Times of London and The National Graphical Association ultimately came to the same issue: who should operate the new computerised equipment. The NGA agreed to accept the equipment if the company were to agree that only NGA members will operate it.[6] Similarly, a regional vice-president of the International Typographical Union explained to the author that electronic technology has had the effect of moving the typesetting process from the backroom to the front office. If members of his union were to be trained and moved from the backroom to the front office, conflicts will be reduced significantly.

In all these cases the difficult problem was not limited to the employment security of workers whose jobs were affected. Indeed, satisfactory employment arrangements would probably have been made with only limited conflict. But, any arrangements which would have phased out the skills, would have also phased out their organisations. This was expressed very succintly by the president of the International Brotherhood of Locomotive Firemen and Enginemen of the United States in testimony before a Canadian Conciliation Board:

> We charge the CPR with wilfully exacerbating relationships by injecting and demanding priority for their demand to remove firemen from diesel locomotives. . . . The very livelihood of our members, the continuation of our craft, and *the continued existence of our organisation are at stake*. . . . This means that firemen are to give up their jobs, see their craft die and *their organisation disappear*. These are not negotiable demands.[7]

Such attitudes should be anticipated from unions whose existence becomes threatened by technological changes. It should not be expected that such unions will readily negotiate their own demise. A different approach would have to be taken in the negotiation of conditions for the implementation of technological changes in such instances, than the approach taken when the existence of the organisation is not being threatened.

The quality of union leadership is critical to the process of technological change, and the nature of adjustments to it. The policy choices that union leaders make can effect employment significantly, yet escape responsibility for it. For example, a contraction in employment can result from inadequate capital investment, from failure to employ modern technology, or from inadequate demand for the product. But, inadequate demand may result from high per unit costs, which may be the result of inadequate capital investment and failure to employ modern technology. Thus, opposition to new technology, and delays in the introduction of modern processes, can result in high per unit costs and high prices, which will bear down on demand and production.

This is not the sort of relationship that workers commonly associate with the policy choices of their union leaders. In the minds of most workers demand for the product or service is market determined, and development of the market is a managerial responsibility. It is unlikely that many of them will associate the decrease in demand with decisions taken regarding the introduction of modern technology. In such case, union leaders responsible for holding back the technological change remain secure in their positions, ostensibly fighting for security of employment.

By contrast, a decrease in employment that results from technological change is more visible and can be related directly to the change in technology. A decision to acquiesce and cooperate with management in the introduction of technology which has negative employment effects places the leadership in a defensive position. They must justify the policy-decision to those who are adversely affected, and must allay the concerns of the membership at large regarding the effects of anticipated future technological changes on employment and skills. Clearly union leaders who choose to cooperate with management in the introduction of technological changes have a more difficult task than those who choose to oppose it.

Microelectronic technology dictates a comprehensive overall approach to its employment effects, not an approach that is limited to the employment functions of an individual worker or to employment in an individual firm or industry. Unlike electromechanical instruments and processes whose effects on employment and skills are for the most part limited to the point or place of application, the effects of microelectronic technology can be widespread. The technology is pervasive in application, and the convergence of computers and telecommunications systems into telematic networks implies nationwide and worldwide effects by the simple act of establishing a link to an established network. This new reality was given recognition by Britain's Trade Union Congress (TUC) in a policy statement urging unions to approach the issue of technological change jointly: the negotiating process, it said, 'should embrace the largest possible proportion of the workforce since technological developments which initially affect only one work group may eventually have implications for the entire workforce'.[8]

This suggests a need for consultation and cooperation amongst unions in their approaches to negotiation on technological issues, and coordination in responses to the challenges of emerging microelectronic processes. The pervasiveness of the technology and the highly diffusive effects of telematic networks, dictate a more active role for coordinating bodies of employee organisations. The alternative to coordination is probably amalgamation of employment-related organisations.

The Trade Union Congress (TUC) advised unions in 1979 to negotiate 'Technology Agreements' with provisions for (a) the amelioration of negative effects on employment and skills, (b) involvement in the decision-making process, preferably at the design stage or at the stage of choice amongst alternative technological systems, (c) the distribution of benefits that will arise from the new technology, and (d) the organisation and control of work processes, and issues related to health, safety, job satisfaction, scheduling of work, work loads, and such other.[9] By mid-1981, some 100 such agreements were negotiated in Britain, with important provisions for protection of jobs, the grading of employees, training, health, machine monitoring of work and shift-work.[10] It is instructive to note, that 93 per cent of the agreements involved white-collar workers.

A new epoch is setting-in which will change dramatically the nature of work processes, worker-work relationships, forms of business and institutional organisation, and forms and methods of governance. The labour intensity of production processes will continue to decrease, probably at an accelerated rate, and participation in work can be expected to become more discontinuous. The pattern of participation in effect heretofore, involving 40–50 years of continuous employment through a lifetime and then retirement, will become increasingly incompatible with emerging attitudes towards work,[11] and increasingly unnecessary from the standpoint of production of the national output and the maintenance of increasing living standards. As micro-electronic technology increases productivity and the ability to pay, interruptions in work participation without severance in employment contracts, for vacations, sick leaves, educational and training leaves, sabbaticals, maternity leaves, and discretionary time off will likely increase in frequency and duration. These potential changes in the organisation of work processes and in worker-work functional relationships, will dictate very significant changes in contractual relationships between workers and the enterprises that employ them.

A number of very important questions arise: can unions influence the uses to which microelectronic instruments and processes will be put and the ways in which the uses will be effected? A. B. Cherns writes:

> different societies will make different use of the microprocessor, which has as much capacity for divergence as convergence: some societies will use the microprocessor to enhance humanistic values, while others will use it to strengthen the domination of individuals by institutions, including work organisation and the state itself.[12]

Who will make the choice? How will the choice be made? Who will participate in the decision-making process? What factors will be taken into account in making the choices? Will trade unions be able to make a case for their participation in the decision-making processes?

It is widely recognised that microelectronic instruments and processes will effect everyone, regardless of the nature of work activity in which people engage. A video-display terminal hooked to a computer, in the store, in the bank, at home or in the office will effectively supervise everyone who operates the terminal and accesses the computer. The computer will monitor the performance of operators, note the times of access, the information that is taken out and put in, the nature of requests that have been made, the requests that have been met, the requests that have been denied, with times and reasons for denial. Who will set the pace of work? Who will deal with the implications of the monitoring process? With whom will employees argue their cases when not able to argue with their microelectronic supervisor? Who will be the intermediary? If employees are to be protected against decisions of 'supervisors' with whom they cannot argue their cases verbally, then employee organisations will have to ensure the existence of processes which provide for human intervention.

It is possible that management may be more willing to cooperate on this issue than it has been in relation to the introduction and consequences of other technologies in the past. Unlike other technologies, microelectronic technology has the potential to effect the functions of management even more than the functions of some other employees. In reality, for the first time in the history of technology, management may find itself under continuous supervision. Microelectronic instruments and processes have the capacity to monitor the work of managers, to assess management decisions on the basis of the available evidence, to suggest alternative decisions, to recommend promotions, demotions and transfers, to select personnel for projects and functions, to prod, to caution, to reprimand and to encourage. Management will find itself compelled to formulate arguments against the recommendations that will flow from the computer systems. The computer may say, for example, that on the basis of the information deposited with it regularly and routinely by government agencies, research organisations, and financial institutions, the investment decision contemplated by management should not be undertaken. The onus will be on management to show why it should go ahead.

What is happening in reality is that computers are becoming interlopers between the company and management, in the way unions became interlopers between companies and their employees. As a result, management may become increasingly sympathetic to the concerns of employees. It is not uncommon for adversaries to bind together in the face of a common threat. This development highlights a reality of modern industrial organisation that is often forgotten: namely, that management are employees, too. Most managers are not owners of the enterprises they manage. They are not the employers; the enterprises are the employers. Managers are salaried employees, vested with decision-making powers on behalf of the enterprises they are hired to manage. They are hired, fired, promoted, transferred, demoted like any other employee. Indeed, organised employees, whose employment is governed by terms and conditions set out in binding contracts, may have greater security of employment, and greater certainty about the nature of functions they will be asked to perform than do management employees. What will happen to them when computers become vested with powers to protect the interests of the enterprise, and are given the capacity to make discriminatory decisions on the basis of all the available evidence? How will management react when the computer states 'on the basis of the evidence available to us, this or that decision should not have been made'; or 'on the basis of the information provided to us, X should have been promoted not Y'. Management may increasingly find itself questioned, reprimanded, and called to account. It may find that personality variables which influenced management decisions, such as forcefulness, likability, friendship and blood, school tie and fraternity, effective presentation of arguments, and arrogance are no longer of consequence when logic becomes the dominant element in decision-making processes. What will happen when subjectivity is removed from the decision-making process? The outcome may well be the organisation of management employees into bargaining units. It is not inconceivable for unions of workers and unions of management to join together to fight against whoever will exercise control over the microelectronic systems.

5 Development and Application of Technology

Opinions vary widely on the factors that influence the development and application of technology. There is general agreement that most technologies, even the most radical ones, originate from efforts to introduce minor improvements in the performance of existing technologies; and there is general agreement, also, that market developments *induce* the development and application of technology. Examples should abound: in the historical past, the water pump was a necessary technological solution to water problems in underground mining; development of the telegraph was essential to the running of the railways; the development of two-way wireless communication was essential to the flying of aircraft; and development of the cotton gin was induced by the development of textile machinery that used cotton instead of wool. In more recent times, the increase in the price of oil induced the development of technology for the exploitation of alternative energy sources, such as, heavy oil, shale oil, solar energy and coal gasification, and equally, induced the development and application of technology designed to increase the power yield per unit of input and thereby reduce consumption.

Dudley Dillard comments that 'Technological change is interdependent, cumulative, and irreversible.'[1] It is *interdependent* in the sense that its application in one activity stimulates application in other activities, and its efficient use in one activity depends on the use of specific technologies in other activities. The steam engine stimulated the development of the steam boat, the steam locomotive, and the steam turbine; the sewing machine revolutionised tailoring, shoemaking, hat making, and the leather goods industry; and 'Wilkinson's boring machine enabled Watt to bore round cylinders for his steam engine.'[2] Microelectronic technology is still at the experimental stage of development. Its application to date has been in the nature of the application of space technology – selective probing. We know that it will revolutionise production processes throughout the economic and social infrastructure, and that new industries, processes, products and services will spring up, but when, where, what kinds, we do not really know.

Technological change is *cumulative* in the sense that one development leads to another, and every succeeding development is based on some elements of developments that preceded it. 'Nearly every so-called invention' writes Dillard 'derives from a knowledge of prior inventions . . . invention is a social process in relation to which the contribution of any single individual, no matter how great his genius, is relatively small'.[3] This reality emphasises the critical importance of the wide dispersion of information on technological development. Secrecy limits the range of inquiry, and stifles the developmental process.

Finally, technological change is *irreversible* because its application compels the development of processes and organisational structures that are irreversible. Large scale machine technology dictated the establishment of large scale production processes, which, in turn, dictated the formulation of large business organisations. A question of considerable consequence is what kinds of production processes and forms of organisation will be dictated by microelectronic technology. Dillard writes: 'Technological imperatives not only make economic developments irreversible, but they limit the choices available at any time and thus impart a degree of determinism to the future course of economic development.'[4] To-date, the application of microelectronic instruments has not had any pronounced effects on processes and forms of organisation, largely because in most instances they have been used as individual instruments, i.e. as stand alone computers, word processors, and such, rather than as elements in integrated production processes. As indicated above, the replacement of the typewriter with a word processor will not change the production process of an office significantly, just as the use of a computer for data processing will not change the organisational structure of the enterprise. But, the link of the word processor to the computer, and the establishment of an interactive network of micro-computers, video display terminals, and other microelectronic instruments within organisations, will impact significantly on both the production processes and the forms of organisation.

The Rate of Application

The development of a technology does not mean, of course, that its application to production processes will be rapid. The rate of application depends on many factors amongst which cost-effectiveness, demand for the goods or services produced by the technology relative to its capacity to produce, and the availability of investment capital are important factors. Manufacturers and distributors of microelectronic instruments and processes will attest that the rate of application worldwide in 1982 was significantly lower than in 1980, because demand for goods and services has fallen and investment capital has become more scarce.

The rapid and widespread application of electronic technology to production processes forecast twenty years ago was based largely on the following: (a) significant improvement in the technology of computers, which would make individual units less cumbersome than the early models; (b) decreases in computer prices, which would make computers and computer-related instruments accessible to smaller institutions and enterprises, and thereby expand the market for them; (c) increases in computer services, which were expected to bring about lower prices and costs; and (d) the development of a wider range of software, which were expected to facilitate computer applications to a wider range of activities. All of these developments have taken place in varying degrees. Yet, the spread has not been as substantial as it was expected.

Now, there is a renewal of exaggerated expectations, based largely on the advent of *microelectronics*. This new phase of the electronic 'revolution' is expected to find very rapid and very widespread application in all production processes as well as in consumer durables. Amongst the most frequently cited characteristics which are supposed to cause acceleration in application there are the following:[5]

1. Microelectronic instruments and processes are appropriate for the performance of a wide range of service activities which heretofore have been largely or entirely labour intensive, such as clerical, retail, and other.
2. The small size of microelectronic chips makes them appropriate for insertion into most consumer durables.
3. The technology is relatively cheap, and it is expected to become cheaper.
4. It is exceptionally reliable and precise in the activities it performs.
5. It is all pervasive.
6. It has a universal range of application.
7. It is developing on an international scale, which means it will become abundant in supply.
8. It is environmentally benign.
9. Its size and cost means access to it by individuals and the smallest of enterprises.
10. It has the capacity to both extend and displace a wide range of intellectual and intuitive skills.

In addition to these characteristics, which are expected to facilitate widespread application of microelectronics, impetus to application is expected from the following:

1 Inability of enterprises to undertake the production and distribution of certain goods and services with existing technology and existing processes. The computer facilitated the production of goods and services which were not even conceived possible prior to its introduction; on-line transmission of information established new possibilities for services; and microelectronics is conceived as opening up further possibilities for the production of goods and services.
2 Inability to meet potential demand with existing processes. The capital–labour ratios in existence within individual processes impose limitations on the volume of output that can be produced. In the absence of new technology, output can only be increased through increments in capital and labour. Enterprises encounter limitations on the extent to which they can add successive increments. The technology will facilitate an increase in the volume of output without a proportionate increase in production facilities and manpower.
3 There is a need for instruments and processes which can be applied to activities requiring greater precision than can be obtained with existing processes. Programmed performance is expected to provide such precision.
4 Increasing competition in both domestic and international markets dictates, (a) greater consistency in product quality, and (b) faster response to orders.
5 The reduction of down-time and wastage dictate the introduction of more effective process control.
6 Enterprises face a compelling requirement for more efficient management of inventory.

Exaggerated Expectations

These characteristics and pressures notwithstanding, the technology is not yet at a stage of development which would suggest imminent takeoff. Electronic instruments and processes for individual activities and groups of activities will continue to be introduced, but it will take a long time for the instruments and processes to evolve into a comprehensive electronic infrastructure similar to the electromechanical infrastructure in effect at present.

Most of the agitation about the imminence of widespread use of electronic instruments, processes and systems emanates from vested interests: manufacturers and distributers seeking to create the impression that the final stage in the development of the technology has been reached, and, that, therefore, failure to invest in it now will place one at a competitive disadvantage in the market place; scientists and technologists seeking increases in the allocation of funds for research and development emphasising the imminence of the nation falling behind other countries, even though the probability of staying behind may be very high regardless how much money they are given for the pursuit of their research activities; government bureaucrats in departments and agencies concerned with various aspects of the technology and its economic and social implications agitating to induce increases in budget allocations to them, so that they can expand the range of their activities and increase their prominence within the bureaucracy; individual writers creating a state of agitation to induce an increase in sales of the things they write; and various organised groups, such as labour organisations and organisations of women exploiting the uncertain outcome of electronic application to gain rights and privileges which they have sought for some time. For example, the possible threat to employment in offices, which may effect largely female employees, is being used as a basis for demands to promote more women to managerial positions, which are deemed to be less vulnerable.

Integrated electronic systems, similar to the telephone, telegraph and television systems in existence at present, are 'visible' throughout the nation and the world, but in the distant future. Automated production, distribution and communication systems are a scientific and technological reality. What is not known is the distance of the future. To anxious agitators, the future is tomorrow; allowing no time for all the social, economic and political accommodations that are dictated by the on-coming technological infrastructure. To people who know the state of the technology, the rate at which it is applied, the changes that are taking place and the difficulties that are encountered in applications to different processes, the future is at a considerable distance.

In addition to scientific and technological variables, the rate of application will be influenced by the rate of economic growth. A period of sustained economic growth and expectations of continuing growth are necessary conditions for investment into new technological systems. Existing economic conditions and projected conditions for the balance of this decade suggest a slower rate of application than that recorded during the decade of the 1970s.

There is no doubt that we are moving towards integrated production –

distribution–communication electronic systems. Most electronic instruments in use at present are obsolete in the context of integrated systems, and most electronic processes are rather untidy and inefficient. The word processors that will survive the process of office integration will be only those which have the technical capacity to communicate with computers, other word processors and terminals. Most word processors in use at present do not have such a capacity. Processes are 'untidy' in the sense that they consist of one central processor and several peripherals – input and output terminals, tape stores, printers, etc – scattered around and dependent on the processor for their operation; and they are 'inefficient' because entire network operations depend upon the operative efficiency of the central processor. When the central processor stops, the entire system comes to a standstill.

Efficiency considerations dictate that entire electronic systems – central processor, minicomputers and peripherals – be linked together into integrated interactive networks. The advent of microprocessors makes possible the transformation of peripherals from dependent dummy devices into intelligent, independent, interresponsive system instruments. Such transformation will involve considerable redundancy of dummy electronic instruments and devices currently in use. The history of technological change suggests that the rate of application is considerably faster when the replacement involves people than when it involves capital instruments. This suggests that applications over the foreseeable future will likely be *faster* in labour intensive processes than in capital intensive processes – offices and other service activities, than manufacturing.

The Application of New Technology

We have noted that the rate of application of computers and computer-related systems has been considerably slower than projected. Over time, the exaggerated expectations gave way to the reality that the computer was an instrument which could perform a wide range of functions substantially faster than mechanical and electromechanical processes, and it could perform many functions which could not be performed by conventional processes, but that it was, nevertheless, an instrument, partly complementary to existing instruments and factors, partly supplementary, and a substitute for capital and labour in varying magnitudes. Applications have not been as widespread as expected, and the employment effects have not been as negative as projected. Indeed, on balance the effects on employment appear positive: new occupations and employments have been created, which remain in short supply even after thirty years of operation; and there is no evidence that computer applications have destroyed more jobs than they have created.

The following considerations are cited in decisions to invest or to postpone investing in electronic processes:

State of the art

The availability of *appropriate* technology is a major consideration in investment decisions. Even though much is being said about the advanced state of microelectronic technology, and the actual and potential state of automated processes, there continues to be considerable uncertainty about their operational efficiency. In addition, an element of uncertainty exists in relation to the state of the art itself: this is a period of rapid conversion of inventions into innovations, and innovations into applied processes. The continuous flow of 'improved' instruments, and the resultant obsolescence of the standard ones which may have come on the market only a few months earlier, create uncertainties about the wisdom of investing in them. Hence, decisions tend to be postponed until the technology attains a degree of innovative stability. Consider, for example, the employment of industrial robots: a variety of them have existed for many years, and the industries that produce them have made valiant efforts to induce their employment. But there have been uncertainties about what they can do, how much they can do, and how efficiently they can be used. In addition, the continuous flow of information on improvements in them cause potential employers of them to postpone their purchase until the ultimate 'perfect' unit is produced. The signals from industry now are that the ultimate have been produced, and it is expected that the employment of industrial robots will takeoff. A representative of International Resource Developmemt (IRD) is quoted to have declared: 'After fifteen years of slow and painful growth the market for industrial robots is about to explode.' He attributed this anticipation to the fact that the new generation of industrial robots have 'greatly improved adaptive capabilities, so that a robot can deal with abnormal, as well as expected circumstances'. But, having extolled the virtues of the new generation, he proceeded to predict the evolution of heuristic robots, i.e. 'those which will learn from experience how to do their job better'.[6] Herein will be found the basis for reluctance to invest in them at this time. As long as there continue to exist indications of significant improvements in equipment and processes, there will continue to exist reluctance to commit investment capital to currently available technology. That is, as long as the application of innovations threatens to render the modern obsolete within a brief period after its installation, potential users will postpone its purchase until that threat diminishes somewhat. In the meantime, they will lease, rent, and purchase only those parts of the process which are least likely to be rendered obsolete by changes in technology.

Anticipated demand

The rate at which inventions become innovations and innovations are converted into operational systems depends to a considerable degree on the anticipated demand for the goods and services to be produced by the systems. The demand for factors of production is a *derived* demand. It is derived from the demand for the goods and services they produce. It follows that uncertainty about the level of demand for goods and services, or uncertainty on whether a desirable level of demand can be sustained over a period which would make the undertaking profitable, implementation will likely be postponed. For example, one of our leading enterprises indicated last year that the implementation of a CAD/CAM system was 5–6 years away. The system is now operational. The 5–6 years was reduced to 5–6 months when the introduction of the system became a condition for the successful satisfaction of a potential demand within a specified period of time. On the other hand, another enterprise which had made a tentative decision to proceed with the introduction of an automated process postponed implementation indefinitely when it was determined that the rate of increase in demand was too low relative to the potential capacity of the process.

Also, changes in relative prices bear on demand, and thereby stimulate innovative activity in the production of the goods and services effected. For example, in recent years there has been increasing substitution of self-service production processes for labour intensive market processes at gasoline stations, restaurants, retail stores, banks, and many other establishments. Indications are that this process of substitution will continue. In addition, increasing numbers of durable goods and production equipment are being so designed as to facilitate their repair without the use of specialised services.

In some operations, such as those in the telephone industry and in financial institutions, the introduction of labour-saving techniques is incidental to the search for ways to do things that could not be done by conventional methods, and to expand the volume, variety and speed of services without significant increases in costs and prices. Some of the services that are being provided by electronic technology were not feasible technically with the use of electromechanical processes, and some could not have been provided at price ranges that would fall within potential demand. The need for greater volume, wider variety and greater speed in the provision of banking and telecommunications services was long recognised. The problems were technical feasibility and cost. The invention and application of electronics solved the technical problems and the rapid increase in demand for the services solved the cost-price problem. The services are being provided at price ranges that indicate substantial increases in demand, which provides stimulus to continuous application of new technology.

Generally, the most rapid rates of electronisation can be expected in establishments which cannot meet the increasing demand for their goods or services with their existing production processes.

Changes in materials and products

Related to anticipated demand are changes in materials and products. Frequently, investment in new equipment is dictated by changes in the design and nature of products, and changes in the materials used. For example, the reasons commonly cited for decisions to invest in computer-directed numerically controlled machines are: (a) the labour-operated semi-automatic mechines cannot work on the new metals that are required for some products; (b) the precision work that is required is beyond the capacity of the worker-instrument-machine combinations in existence; and (c) the NC machines have the capacity to switch automatically from one work specification to another, which reduces the down-time associated with changes in parts and retooling.

Labour costs, supply of labour, labour-management relations

Frequent reference is made to labour costs as an explanatory variable in decisions to automate. Excessive increases in wages relative to productivity, increasing paid holidays, sick leave and statutory holidays, employer contributions to health plans, dental plans, pension plans, disability insurance, increasing rates of absenteeism and turnover, and decreasing labour efficiency, are viewed as negative to the employment of labour. Not only are labour costs rising more rapidly than can be absorbed without adverse effects on product demand and return to investment capital, but also, and more importantly, management appears to have lost control over labour costs. The loss of control is manifested in the substantial increase in the proportion of non-wage labour costs (often referred to as 'the hidden' labour costs), and in the frequent and substantial divergence of actual labour costs from projected labour costs. This renders long range planning increasingly more difficult and increasingly risky, at a time when longer range planning is becoming increasingly more necessary.

J. K. Galbraith asserts that the primary consideration is control over costs of production, which dictates the reduction as much as possible of variable costs. Since labour is a major contributor to variable costs, it follows that the displacement of labour becomes a primary consideration. To quote:

> In its planning, the technostructure seeks to minimise the number of contingencies that are beyond its control. Labour costs and supply are significantly of this character and more so when there is a union. To substitute capital, in the form of machinery, the supply and cost of which are wholly or largely under control, for labour which is not and which can strike, is an admirable bargain.[7]

Undoubtedly, unsatisfactory labour-management relations and labour costs out of control may dictate the taking of deliberate decisions at labour substitution. But, first the substitute technology must be available, and must be proven economically viable. Given the appropriate technology and its economic viability, then the substitution is the result of relative costs, and not the result of the nature of labour-management relations or the degree of management control over costs. It is doubtful that these will be of an overriding consideration if the costs of alternative systems were to be considerably higher.

Nevertheless, given the availability of appropriate technology, labour-related problems, such as, scarcity of specialised workers, restrictive regulations regarding who can perform what work-functions, when, how, and under what conditions, and uncertainty or concern about the rate of increase in labour costs, would tend to stimulate investment in capital intensive processes. Therefore, the quest for substitution of labour with capital is in effect quest for a decrease in the element of uncertainty regarding the availability of manpower, quest for greater stability in the cost structure, and greater certainty about anticipated costs.

Employers of robots have indicated that labour-related issues did enter into their decisions to invest in robots. Scarcity of skilled manpower has been an important consideration: 'We did not automate the process for the sake of automating', declared a respondent to our enquiries. 'We automated in response to difficulties in finding adequate supply of qualified manpower.' Another respondent indicated that the primary consideration was 'the reduction or elimination of variations in hiring caused by variations in production.' Apparently, seasonal variations in production necessitated the hiring of substantial numbers of workers on a temporary basis. Aside from the recurrent problem of finding the required numbers of desirable workers, there was the problem of inexperience and lack of work discipline, which contributed to low productivity, waste, defective output, and high unit costs. It was expected that, amongst other positive contributions to efficiency, 'the electronic system will smooth out the peaks and troughs in hiring'. A third respondent indicated that 'the anticipated increase in business' could not have been achieved with the conventional labour-based processes of production.

An aspect of labour which tends to stimulate continuous search for non-labour contributors to productivity is the nature of labour itself. Human labour faces physiological and social group limitations in the performance of work functions. These limitations constrain the rate of increase in efficiency and impinge on the flexibility of production processes. The limitations are particularly pronounced where the human factor is the key element in the production process. The history of industrial development is replete with examples of efforts to overcome these constraints—time and motion studies, audio-visual studies, motivational studies, group incentives, and many other. But, these have limitations in themselves: even if all individual and social group limitations were to be removed, and human physiology were to function in perfect harmony with technology and the production process, eventually an optimum level of performance would be reached. Improvements in the rate of efficiency beyond that level will only be achieved by complementing the human factor with technical instruments or by the substitution of the human factor with mechanical or electromechanical technology. This suggests that the human factor is in long run disadvantage in competition with technology.

None of our respondents cited changes in relative prices of capital and labour amongst their reasons for investing in automated processes. We know the price of labour has risen steadily over the past 20 years, and we also know that prices of computers and computer-related instruments and processes have declined steadily. Yet, it is not relative prices that are cited for investing or not investing; it is rather the availability of investment capital, the availability of specialised labour, and production-related problem of all kinds. It is possible, of course that relative factor prices enter into decisions implicitly, as when reference is made to quest for increase in productivity to offset rising unit costs, caused largely by rapidly rising wages and salaries. In such case, the consideration is not the price of labour relative to the price of capital taken by themselves; the consideration is rather their relative prices related to productivity. Wages may be high or low. Taken by themselves they mean nothing in relation to productivity. It is very often the case that low wage establishments face greater difficulties to remain profitable than high wage establishments. The explanation will be found in productivity differences. Increases in wages do not necessarily result in higher wage costs. Wage costs may increase, decrease or remain unchanged. The outcome will depend on the volume of output relative to the total wage bill. If the volume of output were to increase by more than the increase in the wage bill, wage costs will decrease. Wages and wage costs are not synonymous, common usage notwithstanding. Wages are transformed into wage costs by the output.

Other motivating factors

References are also made to such factors as the variability and uncertainty of energy and environmental costs, and the anticipated increasing scarcity of known sources of energy as motivating factors for an acceleration in the rate of microelectronisation. Undoubtedly increasingly stringent environmental regulations have stimulated the search for automated processes which would reduce pollution, and the increasing scarcity of conventional oil supplies, has stimulated the search for instruments and processes which will find alternative sources and reduce the consumption of oil. But, users of electronic production processes have not attributed any significance to such factors. Rather, their decisions to invest in electronic equipment appear to have been based on evidence that automated processes facilitate the following (in order of significance):

(a) the production of goods and services which could not have been produced by conventional methods of production;
(b) the development of process-capacity to meet anticipated increase in demand;
(c) increase in efficiency of operations;
(d) shortening of lead time – faster response to customer requests;
(e) easier and more effective inventory control;
(f) greater consistency in product quality;
(g) the precise duplication of products over long periods of time.

An investigation of management decisions in Great Britain to invest in automated technology concluded that the objectives were to achieve greater predictability, reliability, consistency and controlability in operations.[8]

It is often the case that *the rate* at which a new technology is introduced is influenced by its availability, the anticipated improvement in productivity, the promotional activities of producers, the anticipated purchase decisions of competitors, the availability of investment capital, and anticipated demand for the services being produced and to be produced. Producers and distributors of new technology have tended to exaggerate the potential benefits in terms of the nature of work to be done, and the quantity and quality of output to be produced, and minimised the cost implications for the organisation of work processes, worker-work relationships, quality and skill mix of the manpower complement, and other variables that enter into the adjustment process.

The rate is also influenced by the education and training of those associated with the operational efficiency of the technology. A rate faster than the time it takes to train and retrain the people involved in its operation will result in the underuse and misuse of the technology. Much computer power has been wasted over the past 30 years by the relentless emphasis on computer hardware and the virtual neglect of the critical element required for the operational efficiency of computers, which is the supply of software specialists. A computer without a programme is like a pocket calculator without a battery. Yet, little effort was put by producers of hardware to facilitate an increase in the supply of software and software specialists.

The relatively slow rate of software production appears to have slowed down the rate of computer utilisation more than the rate of computer installation. Producers and distributors of computers appear to have convinced users that experimentation with alternative ways of computer operation is part of the process of using computers. They have made the underuse and misuse of computer technology an acceptable reality. Yet, the reality is that the inefficient use is related to the imbalance between computer applications and the supply of software specialists. The increasing realisation by users that they bear avoidable costs, is resulting in actions designed to correct the imbalance. Many have delayed the installation of computer systems until they determine precisely what functions are to be performed, and whether the required software and software specialists are available. The development of appropriate software is increasingly preceding the purchase of the hardware.

Another labour-related issue which bears on the rate of introduction and utilisation of microelectronic technology is the equipment-manpower ratio. Early productivity estimates were based on the assumption that an operator of a word processor or a video display terminal will interact with the equipment continuously during the regularly scheduled work day. We have now found that an operator can interact efficiently with a video display terminal over relatively limited periods of concentrated work. Aside from widely reported allegations of health problems, which have undoubtedly caused some psychosomatic illnesses, we have determined that prolonged periods (in excess of one hour) of concentrated reading off the video screen reduces efficiency in both reading and concentration. All evidence suggests that the efficient utilisation of video display terminals attended by operators on a one-to-one basis will require the scheduling of relatively short work-shifts. This has important implications for the organisation of work, and even perhaps for employment. More part-time employment is suggested.

From the standpoint of employment generally, the rate of a major technological change such as microelectronics should be related to the rate of general economic growth. In the absence of general growth and when the rate of growth is very low, there is no net addition to total economic and social activity. Disappearing and declining enterprises and activities are barely offset by emerging enterprises and activities. The labour force displaced by the new technology and much of the increase in the labour force cannot be provided with alternative employments. Economic growth and rising real incomes create and facilitate the creation of work activities. To the extent that new technology contributes to economic growth it creates general employment, even though oftentimes it displaces labour at the point of the production process where it is applied.

Faster Microelectronisation of Offices and Service Activities

The rate of microelectronisation has been faster in offices and certain service activities, such as banking, than in goods-producing processes, and indications are that the faster rate will continue over the foreseeable future. A number of explanations can be given for this development, amongst which the more important are the relatively low productivity of most office and service processes, and the output limitations of processes that are predominantly labour intensive.

Goods-producing processes are largely capital intensive, and present no serious productivity problems at *the production level* of operations. The problems will be found in the largely labour intensive processes in offices and service activities, which often neutralise productivity improvements at the production level. It is not an infrequent occurrence of positive efforts at the production level of operations to become negative results in the balance sheet because of inefficiencies in areas of activity removed from the production level. It follows, then, that if productivity improvements at the production level of operations are to be sustained, efficiency must increase in areas of operational activity that tend to drag it down, namely, in offices and generally labour intensive service activities.

The second explanation for the faster microelectronisation of office and service activities will be found in the limits they impose on the rate of expansion in both goods-producing and services-producing processes. The labour intensity of service processes, and the largely manual ways in which work activities are performed in them, impose limitations on the rate at which some services can be expanded, and on the nature and range of services that can be provided. For example, it is problematical whether banks and other financial institutions would have been able to expand their services to the extent that they have in the absence of electronic processes. The rapid expansion of service sector activities over the past two decades, and the concomitant expansion of employment in it, created some serious bottlenecks in both the sector itself and in the economy generally, which manifested themselves in inefficiencies and rising costs. The bottlenecks were arresting the rate of expansion in both services-producing and goods-producing industries. Therefore, there emerged a critical need for the restructuring of services-producing processes. The advent of electronics, and the development of electronic equipment appropriate to services-producing activities, may be viewed as a technological response to a crisis in the development of the modern economy.

The third explanation, noted earlier but warranting repetition is in the change in relative prices of capital and labour in recent years. As long as the supply of labour for service activities remained plentiful at prices that were lower than the prices of capital instruments that could have been used instead, processes remained largely labour intensive. In other words, there was no incentive to develop and invest in technology as long as there was a comparative advantage to employ labour. Where the price of labour relative to the price of capital gave an advantage to capital, as for example, in railway transportation, telephone communication, and electrical utilities, appropriate technology was developed and capital intensive processes were established. In recent years, rising wage and salary costs in most service sector activities stimulated a search for capital instruments and processes to increase productivity and reduce the need for more labour. Coincidental with the increase in wages and salaries the prices of some microelectronic instruments decreased.

The combined effect of the opposite movement in relative prices of capital and labour has been to weaken significantly the comparative advantage of labour.

A fourth and major reason will be found in the confluence of the nature of activities performed in offices and services-producing processes and the capabilities of microelectronic technology. Computers, telecommunications technologies and other electronic instruments are designed to receive information, store it, manipulate it, retrieve it, analyse it, and transmit it. Most of the activities performed in offices and services-producing processes are of the same nature—compiling storing, analysing, retrieving and communicating information. Clearly, microelectronic technology is very appropriate for office and services-producing activities.

The implications of these for employment and skills are examined elsewhere in this book. Suffice to say here that many labour intensive processes in offices and services-producing establishments will become increasingly capital intensive, and employment in them will inevitably follow the pattern established in goods-producing processes as they changed from labour intensive to capital intensive. There are services, of course, such as people to people services which by their very nature will remain labour intensive. But, as we already experience in hospitals, schools, and even recreational activities many aspects of people to people services, too, can be performed efficiently and effectively by electronic processes. It is time for a general recognition that the age of labour intensive production processes is coming to an end. Such a recognition will perhaps set in motion policy formation processes and the establishment of programmes that will accommodate the change, with a minimum of adverse effects on those who will be affected. The process of change has been relatively slow, and it is likely to remain relatively slow over the next two decades. This presents a welcome opportunity to plan and implement effective accommodative social, political and economic programmes.

6 Occupations and Occupational Structure

Introduction

Technological changes are an important element in the distribution of the labour force amongst industries and sectors of the economy, and have a significant influence on the occupational structure. The decrease of employment in agriculture over the past 30 years, and the constancy in the proportion of the labour force employed in manufacturing are generally attributed to technological changes. Similarly, the very substantial changes that have been recorded in the occupational structure over time are generally attributed to the effects of changing technology on the functional content of jobs, and to the changes in knowledge and skills that such changes compel.

At the outset it is desirable to examine the meaning of the term 'occupation,' and *how occupations* and *occupational structures* change.

An occupation (or employment classification) is a specified range of work functions related to a given process of production. An engineer's occupation is associated with a range of general engineering work functions, and a range of specific work functions that are related to the engineer's specialisation – mechanical, chemical, electronic, nuclear, and other. An engineering technician's occupation is associated with another range of work functions, some of which may overlap with the professional engineer's work functions. The typist has a range of work functions, and so does a clerk. These, too, often overlap.

Technological changes, whether they be in the form of a new machinery and equipment, changes in the organisation of production processes, new materials and products or increases in technical knowledge, affect occupations through their effects on the work functions associated with them: some of the functions are eliminated, new functions are added and some functions are transferred from one occupation to another. When some of the work functions of an occupation are removed from it, either because they are no longer needed in the production process, or because they are performed with equal efficiency and at lower cost by some other occupation, or because they have been embodied into mechanical or microelectronic instruments and processes, employment in the occupation will decrease, unless the occupation undertakes the performance of some other work functions or the volume of work produced by the occupation increases so much as to offset the decrease in work functions. All occupations undergo functional changes over time: new knowledge is displacing old knowledge; work done manually in the past, is being done with the assistance of instruments or by instruments; work that was being done is no longer done; and work is being done with the assistance of mechanical and microelectronic instruments that could not have been done without their assistance.

Defining an occupation as 'a range of work functions' is closer to the reality of employment, than would be the traditional association of occupations with single work activities. The number of occupations and employment classifications that are limited to single work functions is relatively small. This is why adjustments to technological changes have become routine: when there is only one work function, the elimination of it means the elimination of the occupation; this would cause a major occupational adjustment; but, when there is a range of functions, the elimination of some of them does not eliminate the occupation; rather, it would cause a re-arrangement of work functions.

The *occupational structure* of the labour force is made up of the thousands of occupations and grades of occupations employed throughout the economy – managerial and administrative, professional, technical, sales, clerical, occupations employed in manufacturing, construction, transportation and communication, agriculture and in scores of activities related to personal and business services. Technological changes impact on the occupational structure through (a) the creation of new sets of work functions; (b) increases in the range of work functions of established occupations, requiring the separation and transference of some work functions to new occupations; (c) the substitution of technological innovations for manpower; and (d) the dilution of skills by complementary technological innovations.

New sets of work functions (new occupations) are created by new products, new processes and increases in knowledge. In addition, increases in knowledge that relate to the activities of specific occupations may result in the formation of separate sets of work functions, and the creation of new occupations or different grades of the same occupation. In either case the number of occupational categories tends to increase.

For example, a few decades ago, the nurse was responsible for duties which since have been taken over by X-ray technicians, laboratory technicians, dieticians, medical social workers, medical records clerks, physical and occupational therapists, respiratory technicians, surgical technicians, ward clerks, and others.[1]

On the other hand, it is well known that in many instances knowledge renders knowledge redundant. New knowledge can be equally a complement and a substitute to existing knowledge. To the extent that it is a substitute, it may cause the elimination of some occupations; to the extent that it is complementary it may dilute the skill component of the occupation and thereby facilitate the performance of work functions by relatively unskilled individuals. In such a case, the complementary knowledge causes the substitution of one occupation (relatively skilled) with another (relatively unskilled).

Computers and computer-related electronic systems impact on both the nature of work and the range of work functions. The computerisation of accounting systems, to which reference was made above, reduced the work functions that relate to the recording of entries, balancing accounts, calculating, and the preparing of financial statements. At the same time, the improved access to information, and the automatic generation of a wide variety of statistical and informational configurations facilitated the allocation of more time to work functions that relate to the examination and analysis of information.

Similarly, the computerisation of some clerical work functions, and the introduction of word processors affected the work functions of clerks and secretary–typists: some of them have become operators of word processors; some computer operators; some assumed administrative support functions; and some undertook computer support functions. 'Administrative support' functions commonly involve such activities as the scheduling of meetings, and the collection and organisation of information; whereas 'computer support' functions involve data entry, data control, allocation of computer time, and the distribution of computer outputs.

The introduction of medical information systems in hospitals has permitted pharmacists to drop work functions related to the typing of medication labels, keeping records of prescriptions (by physician, nature of medication, etc.), and compiling reports, and enabled them to expand the work functions that related to the review of medications for possible reactions, consultation with physicians on their patients' medication profiles, and such other professional activities. Similarly, the virtual elimination of clerical work functions in hospital wards, and the almost instantaneous access to patient profiles, enables nurses to expand significantly their patient care functions.

Changes in jobs and changes in job functions are, of course, a very common occurrence in dynamic economies: products disappear, enterprises decline and go out of business, some relocate, and some change the nature and range of products they produce, causing unemployment, relocation of workers, and the erosion of knowledge and skills. An efficient market system will take these displaced and deskilled workers, equip them in the required knowledge and skills, and place them into the new work activities. If the market fails to function efficiently, a lag will develop in the adjustment process which will be reflected in unemployment. In such case, the cause is not the economic change; it is rather the failure of the adjustment process. The existence concurrently of unemployment and vacancies is manifestation of such a situation.

Economic Structure and Occupations

Most activities in which people engage in advanced industrial–commercial economies are information activities – the production, processing and distribution of information.[2] As economies expand, production processes increase in size, number and complexity, incomes increase, the number and variety of goods and services increase, and business, government and institutional bureaucracies expand. The increase in size, number and complexity of enterprises effects various aspects of social functioning, which invite the intervention of governmental agencies: employment standards, health and education standards, municipal services of all sorts, the maintenance of competition, consumer protection, and many other essentially informational work activities are created. In addition, the increase in size of enterprises, whether they are industrial, commercial or institutional, makes planning necessary, whose essence is information. Galbraith expressed to development this way:

> Planning, in short, requires a great variety of information. It requires variously informed men and women who are suitably specialised in obtaining the requisite information. . . . on large and small matters information must be extracted from specialists, tested for its reliability and relevance, and made to yield a decision. . . . The modern business organisation . . . consists of numerous individuals who are engaged . . . in obtaining, digesting or exchanging and testing information.[3]

Also, as the number of producers and products increases, competition intensifies, which gives rise to scores of information jobs in marketing, sales, public relations and advertising. Competition provides buyers with choices; and it is the task of competitors to influence the making of choices. The greater the actual and potential competition, the greater would be the tendency to employ information workers who would produce and disseminate the competing information. This is as true of enterprises as it is of governments which face actual and potential competition. As indicated elsewhere, there is no substantive difference between the advertising agency employed by General Motors and the agitational propagandists employed by the Kremlin. The task of each is to sell a product, and directly or indirectly cause consumers to believe that competing products are inferior substitutes.

The evolution of an information economy, and the concomitant information occupational structure, is in evidence over a period of at least 50 years: the collapse of goods production in the 1930s, followed by the on-set of a war economy in the 1940s and 1950s,[4] changed the structures of industrial societies and industrial economies in ways that emphasised the social aspects of economic activity. The depression and the wars that followed compelled the governments of free enterprise economies to assume responsibility for the ends of economic activity in both the private and public sectors. They enunciated goals in relation to rates of economic growth, full employment, price stability, distribution of income, wages, hours of work, conditions of work, and so on. Although the quest for profit remained the stimulus to activity in private activity, the ways in which the profit was made became a social concern. Government agencies began to watch and probe, union organisations began to protect workers, and voluntary public organisations began to challenge.

The change in economic and social climate brought about an increase in entrepreneurial activity and resulted in a spread out of the enterprise structure. It did not reduce the size and number of large monopolistic and oligopolistic enterprises in steel, transportation, communication, or automaking; on the contrary, many of these increased in size very substantially. What it did was to increase opportunities for entrepreneurial activity, and thereby increase the number of enterprises generally. This resulted in a very substantial increase in the number of players in the market. One of the leading economists of the twentieth century, Joseph A. Schumpeter, put forth the thesis that in capitalist economies the entrepreneur played the leading role in economic development. Investment capital was important, but it was the entrepreneur who sought out investment opportunities, it was the entrepreneur who developed new products, and it was the entrepreneur who developed new techniques, and explored, developed and exploited new resources.[5]

Concurrent with this change in the structure of the economy, incomes increased generally, resulting in an increase of demand for more and greater varieties of goods and services. The production and distribution of rapidly increasing quantities and varieties of goods and services generated demand for a labour force that was distinctly different from the labour force that was engaged in agriculture, mining, forestry, production process manufacturing, and construction. This labour force needed more education, had to be more adept to interpresonal communications, and had to work more with people than with nature and machines.

The rapid expansion of the market, the increasing involvement of governments in economic and social affairs, the increasing participation of organisations—employer and employee organisations, consumer associations, trade organisations, professional associations, international organisations (UN, UNESCO, OECD, EEC) and many other brought about a very substantial growth of information workers: bureaucracies expanded at all levels of government – municipal, state, federal; countervailing bureaucracies emerged and expanded rapidly in private sector industries, institutions, and organisations; bureaucracies in employer organisations stimulated the emergence of bureaucracies in employee organisations; and increasing competition in the market place, and increasing governmental and social challenges, forced industry to increase the numbers of information workers to supply governments with information, to promote products, to improve its historically tarnished image of a ruthless pursuit of profit, and to battle the social challenges. Governments hired lawyers to draft laws, bureaucrats to monitor and administer them, and police officers to enforce them; industry, individuals and groups hired lawyers to find loop-holes in the laws, to avoid and evade penalties, and to defend them in courts of law. The emergence and growth of employee organisations brought about bargaining on terms and conditions of employment, and resulted in the emergence of information occupations engaged in organising employees, managing employee organisations, bargaining, administering collective agreements, arbitrating disputes, administering pension plans, wage and salary structures, employee counselling and interviewing, and so on.

The proportion of the labour force engaged in the production of goods – farmers and farm workers, miners, forestry workers, and production process workers in manufacturing – declined gradually but steadily, and the proportion of workers engaged in the production of services increased rapidly: administrative and managerial, professional and paraprofessional, clerical, sales and service workers became the focus of employment expansion. In individual enterprises the emphasis shifted from the production process to finance and marketing. The automobile industry put more effort and ingenuity into the design and promotion of its product than into its durability and operational efficiency. The production of quality products takes craftsmen – as demonstrated for so many years by the production of the Rolls Royce car. Such a product does not need much organised promotion; it promotes itself; the production, promotion and sales of mass-produced products in competitive markets requires the services of large numbers of information workers – engineers to model them, advertisers to make them appealing, and salesmen to push them. Thus, although mass-production and the availability of huge quantities of goods convey the impression that developed industrial societies are primarily goods-producing societies,[6] they are in fact services-producing societies. Goods-production is a characteristic of preindustrial societies. As industry and commerce develop and expand, incomes increase, and mass-production processes become predominant, increasing proportions of the working population become engaged in service activities.

In *mature* industrial-commercial societies, such as the American, with an advanced mechanical and electromechanical production infrastructure, no more than about 30 per cent of the working population are engaged *directly* in the production of goods. Only about 3 per cent are engaged directly in the production of livestock, grains, vegetables, fruits and other agricultural goods; about 12 per cent are engaged in mining, forestry, other primary activities and construction; and about 15 per cent are engaged directly in the processing and production of manufactured goods. The remainder are engaged in the production of services: some related directly to the production, distribution and sale of the goods, such as managerial, clerical, sales and service, but most not so directly related. They provide general public services, educational services, health and social services, financial services, and so on.

This is the reality of the *mature* mechanically-based industrial – commercial society. The question now arises what will happen in the occupational structure when microelectronic instruments and processes are introduced in the largely labour intensive services-producing activities, and when the mechanical infrastructure is complemented and replaced by microelectronic instruments and processes. Since most of the population is no longer engaged directly in goods-production, further automation of goods-producing processes cannot have a very significant impact on the occupational structure at that level of production. Undoubtedly some occupations will be eliminated, and, the need for other will be reduced in varying degrees, but there is nothing new in that; it has been taking place continuously. Similarly, some goods will disappear from the market-place, which, too, will effect some occupations. But, there is nothing new in this either; it is a common phenomenon in a dynamic economic system. All in all the proportion of the population engaged directly in the production of goods will decrease further. This was happening, and would have continued to happen under a mechanical and electromechanical infrastructure. It is possible that under a mechanical and electromechanical infrastructure the numbers employed directly in the production of goods would have eventually stabilised at some level, as they started to stabilise in agriculture, but nevertheless, until that level were reached a continuing decrease was expected. The introduction of microelectronic instruments and processes will accelerate the decrease somewhat, but that is all.

The major impact on the occupational structure will be felt in the service-producing activities. Both the goods-related service activities and service activities generally will face the sort of impact that goods-producing occupations suffered from the on-set of machine production.

The Vulnerability of Occupations

The vulnerability of occupations and employments to microelectronic instruments and processes depends on the nature of work and the range of work functions they perform. Most vulnerable are occupations and employments whose work functions are *process-specific, narrow, fixed*, and involve some form of physical activity, such as vision, hearing, the use of hands, and routine memory work. For example, the monitoring of processes (visual, hearing, touching), the surveillance of activities, typing, recording, sorting and storing (filing) information, assembling information, calculating, drawing and scheduling information, transporting recorded information, diagnosing functional processes where the range of variables is relatively fixed, and such other. The application of these functional characteristics to occupations and employments will identify those that are most vulnerable: a typist is highly vulnerable because the work functions are process-specific (related to the typewriter) and narrow (typing). Any technology that will remove the typewriter will eliminate the typing occupation, just as recording technologies eliminated the work functions of shorthand specialists. The same will apply to filing clerks, stock clerks, checkers, inspectors, sorters, mail delivery workers, meter readers, watchmen, draftsmen, welders, repair mechanics and machinists, assemblers and operatives, bookkeepers, printers, cashiers, tellers, compositors, and all other occupations and employments whose work functions are relatively fixed, narrow in scope and specific to physical production processes.[7]

Contrast the fixed, process-specific and relatively narrow range of work functions of typists, cashiers and bank tellers to those of personal secretaries: the average personal secretary performs a wide range of functions – research, administration, communication, liaison, public relations, and oftentimes is called upon to act as counsellor, therapist, confidant, and personal assistant. The range of functions is as expansive as the employer wishes to make it. The limit is the ability and willingness to pay; there is no fixed requirement of functions dictated by the nature and organisation of the production process.

There are many occupations that have the capacity to generate work functions. As in the case of secretaries, the limit is the willingness and ability of buyers to pay for the services. A Human Resources Consultant, for example, will perform work functions that relate to the hiring of people (interviewing, testing, selecting), the dismissal of people (severance pay arrangements, transferability, retraining), the organisation of work, motivation, grievance procedures, discipline – the range is unending. Accountants have demonstrated the expansive nature of their work in response to the challenge of computers. All expectations, including the initial expectations of their professional organisations, that the computerisation of accounting and financial processes will impact negatively on the employment of accountants have proven wrong. The profession simply shifted the major part of its work from the manual and routine to the analytical – from the computation of data to financial analysis. In the process, it expanded its work functions by more than the functions that were taken over by computers, and instead of the expected surpluses of accountants it created shortages. Lawyers have done the same; doctors have been offsetting the productivity increases of technology for decades; engineers have always managed to create work for themselves, notwithstanding the fact that most of their time-consuming calculations have been transferred to computers; and public servants at all levels have been the masters of work creation throughout history.

To repeat, the critical issue is the capacity of the economy to pay. Given economic growth and increasing ability to pay, there is almost no limit to the amount of socially desirable work that can be created. Schools can offer more courses; the sizes of classes can be reduced significantly; teaching loads can be reduced; day-care facilities can be increased; kindergarten classes can be reduced; more and better facilities and programmes for the aged can be instituted; recreational facilities and programmes can be expanded; and significant improvements can be introduced in the organisation of political activity at local levels. Given economic growth and the capacity of the economy to pay, the vulnerable occupations and employments will be more than offset by new occupations and employments, as has been the case throughout history. The recent declines in employment opportunities, in education, health, public service and other potentially expansive areas of activity are not a manifestation of saturation in employment in them; it is rather the result of reductions in the allocation of resources to them.

Education and Technology

The relationship between technological changes and the educational and skill qualifications of the labour force has been of continuous concern to educators, workers, policy-makers and manpower planners. The redundancy of knowledge associated with innovations, and the deskilling of work activity associated with the application of technological inventions, have been a constant source of apprehension.

In the absence of technology, there would exist a direct functional relationship between labour input and output; and the labour input-output ratio would tend to be relatively stable over time. Technology breaks this direct functional relationship between labour input and output, and introduces varying degrees of variability in the labour input-output ratio. When an instrument is placed into the hands of a worker, the resulting output no longer reflects the knowledge, experience and efficiency of the worker only; it reflects also the quality and efficiency of the instrument. Indeed, depending on the nature of instrument that is being introduced, it may render redundant some or all the knowledge and experience that the worker possesses, and may require the worker's native intelligence only. We know that some technological changes are substitutes for education and skills; some are complementary to education and skills; and some are partly substitutes and partly complements. The difficulty arises when we attempt to determine the degrees of substitutability and complementarity in relation to individual occupations and employment categories.

The fundamental problem is the existence of only vague relationships between educational requirements and the range of work-functions that are associated with individual occupations. Although most work-functions require some specific knowledge, that knowledge is not necessarily related to the level of education that is set as a minimum qualification for the position that is identified with those work-functions. Disagreements between educators and employers on the relevance of the contents of educational programmes are commonplace. Although employers insist on a university degree, a college diploma, senior or junior matriculation, there is evidence that they are willing to substitute experience for any of them. 'Experience' related to the work-functions involved, which may not necessarily be related to the educational content of the relevant educational programme. Excepting professional and specific technical qualifications, the requirements of degrees, diplomas, senior or junior matriculation must be taken to constitute a general standard, and not an educational content related to the work-functions to be performed.

The 'relevant' of today may well be obsolete tomorrow. Employers do not assume responsibility for obsolescence: they simply discard the obsolete resource, whether it be capital or human. Educational institutions must necessarily take the longer view, and take into account the redundancy effect of changing knowledge. No instant puddings with lables that say 'no good if used more than a month after the production (graduation) date'. Institutions cannot allow short-term interests – of students, business, and even their own – and financial and political expediency to change the educative process from one focusing on human development into one preparing people for work.[8] The work-functions that are in demand today will not be in demand tomorrow. Unless the performer of those work-functions has the capacity to learn new work-functions, there will be no work-functions to perform. The functions performed by computer key-punch operators lasted about 10 years; most of the functions performed by plumbers are being phased out by the introduction of plastic pipes; the functions of typesetters and printers are being performed by computers and computer-related peripheral equipment; the functions of stenographers and telegraph operators have virtually disappeared, and the functions of typists are in the process of disappearing.

Even with professional occupations there exist differences between educational qualifications and the specific knowledge required for the performance of specific work-functions. But, the professional is presumed to have sufficient high level fundamental education in the subject of the profession to be able to grasp the specifics of applications without difficulty and long training. Nevertheless, a problem does exist in establishing a proper relationship between educational qualifications and the specific knowledge requirements of work-processes.[9]

The problem is compounded by the existence of related occupations whose education and work-knowledge are closely related. There is much overlap in work-functions between professional occupations and occupations related to them in the work-process: the work-functions of engineers overlap with some of the work-functions of engineering technicians; some of the work-functions of dentists overlap with some of the work-functions of dental hygienists; physicians perform some work-functions which in many instances are performed with equal efficiency and competence by nurses.

Overlapping work-functions provide some desirable flexibility in work processes: they become the adjustment mechanism that brings about equilibrium when surpluses and scarcities of related occupations coincide. For example, when there is scarcity of engineers and a surplus of engineering technicians, the latter can assume the overlapping work-functions performed by the former. Such a transfer of functions from one occupation to another has the same market effect as an actual increase in supply of and demand for the occupations involved. In the case of the engineer–technician relationship, by transferring some functions to the technician the engineer will be able to perform some engineering functions whose performance was precluded by the shortage in supply of engineers. Clearly, the transference in functions has the effect of an increase in supply of engineers. Similarly, the increase in work-functions to be performed by engineering technicians would represent an increase in demand for engineering technicians. Thus, given a shortage of engineers and a surplus of engineering technicians, the transfer of work-functions from the former to the latter would tend to move both occupations toward positions of market equilibrium.[10]

But the flexibility in work-processes that overlapping work-functions afford, complicate the effort to determine the proper relationship between technological changes and educational and skill requirements. Additionally, the work-functions of most occupations (grades of occupations and employment categories) change continuously in response to changes in knowledge regarding the processes to which they are applied, changes in procedures and techniques, changes in demand for and supply of occupations (and those of occupations potentially utilized as partial substitutes), and changes in wages and salaries. Any and all of these cause adjustments in work processes and redistributions in work-functions amongst occupations and employments.

These developments lead to the following general conclusion: the higher the levels of education relative to the requirements of work-processes, and the greater the flexibility in transference of work-functions among related occupations, the lesser would be the dislocative effect of technological changes. To the extent that the work-functions normally performed by some occupations are below the educational and skill qualifications of those who perform them, the introduction of technological changes which require higher level qualifications would result in the optimal utilisation of existing qualifications. Therefore, from the standpoint of efficient accommodation to and of technological changes, it would be desirable to maintain levels of education and skills that are somewhat higher than what production processes require at any point of time.

Technology and High-Level Manpower

A fundamental characteristic in the relationship between educational requirements and job knowledge is that they are substitutes: generally educational requirements tend to rise when knowledge about a job or a process is limited, and they tend to fall when knowledge increases. This would suggest a tendency for educational requirements to rise in periods of widespread research and experimentation with new technologies, and to fall on the downside of the research cycle and when the new technologies become established in production processes.

An appropriate illustration is provided by the development and use of computers. During the initial phase of their introduction, computers were demonstrated by electronics engineers, and computer programmers were required to have degrees in engineering or mathematics. But, over time, as knowledge about the nature and operation of computers increased, the level of education of computer sales representatives decreased, and high school graduation became adequate qualification for training in computer programming. Similar developments should be expected in relation to the operation of microelectronic systems generally: as knowledge about their operations increases, the level of education required of those involved directly in *operational activities* will tend to decrease. Only when the technology reaches stability in its technical development, the appropriate level of education and skill will be established. Therefore, the levels that are now sought for the multitude of occupations involved should be regarded as largely transitional.

This has important implications for education and society at large: a cycle is introduced which parallels the cycle of innovation. When innovative activity is stimulated, whether in quest of perfecting armaments or by international industrial competition, demand for education will rise to search for and make the unkown known. As long as knowledge remains imperfect the quest for its improvement will sustain demand for relatively high levels of education. When knowledge so improves as to require relatively little education to understand and use the products of research, then both the level and specialisation in education would tend to diminish.

A study of the relationship between education and technological innovations over the lifetime of a product concluded:

> high skilled scientists and engineers are required for development of a product and production process before high volume production can occur. Engineering inputs reach a maximum during installation of high-volume production lines. Less highly skilled engineers, and fewer of them, are needed later for cost-reducing improvements and for problem solving associated with production. As they age products move to organisations with progressively lower average skill levels. Great emphasis is placed on transfer of information from early to later production organisations. The primary function of highly skilled labour in product innovation thus appears to be acquisition of knowledge.[11]

This finding has important implications for highly skilled manpower: the demand for it is directly related to the level and range of innovative activity. Research related to improvements in established innovations does not appear to require the level of expertise nor the numbers required in the course of searching for products and processes. The computer provides another relevant example: subsequent to its initial introduction a series of important improvements were introduced; but important as they were, the established labour force was able to cope with them after only minor instruction. Therefore, if it is important to society to have a pool of highly skilled labour, it would be necessary to maintain a continuous programme of innovative research activity.

Educational Qualifications and Requirements

The past twenty years recorded a progressive and general increase in the levels of education almost everywhere. But, it is difficult to ascertain the extent to which the recorded increases were demand-induced, i.e. the result of actual and anticipated increases in the educational requirements of production processes and of the socioeconomic environment at large, and the extent to which they were the result of an autonomous general increase in the levels of education of the population at large, motivated by a general desire for more education and facilitated by rising incomes.

There is no evidence that the increase in general education was dictated by the requirements of production processes; which suggests that social standards, and the positive association of education with employment, incomes, and advancement within the occupational structure have been the primary incentives.

In technologically advanced economies, most technological changes do not appear to require higher than the prevailing levels of general and technical education. Although most industries require somewhat higher levels of completed formal education today than they did five or ten years ago, the extent to which that is a requirement of their new processes of production and the extent to which they are a response to the fact that a greater number of educated and trained people are available in the market, has not been ascertained. Undoubtedly, some new processes require higher levels of education and skills; and some other require different educational and skill content than the processes they replaced (i.e. electronics instead of electromechanical knowledge and skills); but, most processes do not appear to require any substantially different levels than the range of levels possessed by their current labour forces.[12]

There prevails a general view that in advanced industrial–commercial economies, increasing numbers of workers possess more education than is necessary for the efficient performance of their present job-related work-functions. But, explanations for the apparent requirements–qualifications imbalance vary: a general desire of society at large for more education, regardless of the requirements of production processes, is one explanation; quest for employment security in the long run – the ability to accommodate anticipated changes over time, is another; absence of coordination between the sources of demand for labour (industrial, commercial and institutional employers) and the suppliers of education and skills, is still another; or it is simply a manifestation of the freedom of choice in employment that people can exercise in a free market.

The last explanation pertains to those individuals who elect employments that require lower educational qualifications than they possess, because they do not wish to move, or because they provide greater employment security. In each of such cases it becomes a matter of individual choice whether to sacrifice some of the educational qualifications for higher pay, greater employment security, and the convenience of not having to move, or to sacrifice some or all of these for an employment position suited to the individual's educational qualifications.

From the employer's standpoint, the hiring of people with higher qualifications than required for a given job provides operational flexibility. It facilitates the undertaking of operational activities which require higher qualifications, particularly at times of tight labour markets. Also, oftentimes it becomes necessary to hire people with higher academic qualifications in order to get people with a desired level of demonstrated ability. For example, the requirements of the job may be for a good honours BSc. But, experience has it that good honours BSc's proceed to graduate studies. Therefore, the choice becomes one of hiring someone with a BSc who is less than good or hiring someone with an MSc to get the good BSc. By implication, when demonstrated academic ability is a dominant criterion in the selection of applicants, and the academically proficient tend to seek higher levels of education, employers will hire those with more education and pay for it even though the jobs to which they are assigned may, at the outset, not require it.

In conclusion, a close relationship exists between technological innovations, improvements in technology and the qualifications of the labour force. Systematic innovative activity cannot be sustained in the absence of highly skilled and experienced manpower; and highly skilled manpower cannot be developed and utilised effectively in the absence of innovative activity.

The quality of a nation's high level manpower varies in direct relation to the new knowledge that is being created: new knowledge makes old knowledge redundant; which means that as knowledge about a given process increases the qualifications required for its operation will tend to decrease. Therefore, increase in knowledge tends to have an erosive effect on education and a deskilling effect on work knowledge. The implication of this for the level of education and skill of the labour force is evident: if they are to be sustained at relatively high levels, a continuous generation of new knowledge is necessary.

There is evidence of higher levels of education on the average than industrial processes require. The supply of workers with higher levels of education has risen faster over the past two decades than the requirements of industry. As a result, for some years to come, we may have considerable under-utilisation of personal educational capacity. On the other hand, employers have raised questions about the relevance of the levels and nature of education for production processes. A common complaint is that too many school leavers are inadequately trained in basic reading and writing, and too many demonstrate difficulty with elementary arithmetic. Apparently, too many young workers, with relatively high levels of education demonstrate incapacity to communicate effectively, and to carry out simple arithmetic calculations without their pocket calculators.

We do not yet know the kinds of demands that a microelectronic *infrastructure* will have on the population at large, and the kinds of educational qualifications it will require. Microelectronic instruments and processes in employment to-date suggest a barrel-shaped occupational structure, with about equal proportions at the top and the bottom, and most in the middle. The implication of such distribution for education would be an increase in levels of education on the average.

7 Effects on Occupations and Skills

To determine the possible effect of electronic processes on employment in service activities, it is necessary to first identify in some detail the service activities in which people engage, and then assess the nature and degree of impact electronic processes are likely to have on the performance of those activities. There will remain, of course, the question of new services, as existing services disappear or are modified, but that issue will be examined separately.

The approach used by Porat in the classification of information workers seems to be a good one for the classification of workers in service activities generally:[1]

Knowledge producers

This classification will take in everyone who in whole or in part engages in knowledge-creating activities – Galileo dropping objects of different mass from the leaning Tower of Pisa; Charles Darwin sailing around South America; St Thomas Aquinas, Plato, Aristotle philosophising; Euclid and Einstein theorising; Marx, Freud, Nietzche, Rousseau, Adam Smith, and Tawney interpreting human and institutional behaviour and formulating hypotheses on social and economic relationships; and all those who have and are spending their lifetimes in search of knowledge – natural, physical, biological, medical, social, philosophical, mathematical and other research scientists and technicians, both theoretical and applied.

Collectors, packagers and distributors of information

This classification applies to those who are engaged in the collection of information, the packaging of information into various configurations, and in the dissemination of information. The three functional activities are grouped into one classification because many of the occupational groups and employments involved perform two or all three of the functional activities. For example, a teacher collects information, arranges it appropriately for the class to which it is to be presented, and presents it. On the other hand, an enumerator collects information, a statistician packages it, a market analyst interprets it, and a manager applies it in a marketing decision. Someone in payroll, in the finance department, in the production department, in the marketing department collects statistical information; junior statisticians, economists, book-keepers, organise the information into standard configurations; finance officers (accountants, senior economists, and such other) analyse and interpret; managers apply the information in business decisions. Similarly, a research assistant collects information, an editor selects from it that which is relevant for the intended purpose and puts it together, to be disseminated through a book, newspaper, magazine, radio, television or through a marketing letter. Lawyers search legal decisions, select the relevant ones for each case, and argue the merits of the evidence.

Applicators of information (knowledge)
The classification includes all occupations and employments which use information in the making of work process decisions: managers and administrators; engineering specialists; health care workers, such as doctors, nurses, dieticians, physiotherapists, chiropractors, dentists, pharmacists, clinical psychologists engaged in the application of information to treatment (in contrast to information dissemination in which so many of them engage extensively); agronomists and other agricultural scientific specialists; investigators with decision-making powers; architects and architectural technicians; purchasing agents; arbitrators; judges; government policy-makers; instrument designers; air traffic controllers, aircraft pilots; and such other.

Effects To Be Expected

The functions of the last two occupational groups provide an insight into the nature of things to come, and the nature of effects on the work functions of different occupations and employments. The collection of information, the search and extraction of information for specific purposes, partial analyses of information, and the distribution of information will be carried out by computers and computer-related networks. Air Traffic Controllers and Aircraft Pilots have access to information that is being collected and analysed continuously and instantaneously by computers; their function is to apply that information to the decision-making process, which is, to guide the aircraft in takeoff, landing, the selection of appropriate routes and height levels. Their functions are dispensible or indispensible to the extent only that the computer network can make all those decisions automatically. The question is how much knowledge accumulated through work experience is necessary for the effective use of the information provided by the computer network.

Producers of knowledge are not likely to be effected adversely by developments in electronic technology. On the contrary, the capacity of computers to store information, their capacity to search through stored information and select that which appears relevant for different purposes, and the capacity to perform complex calculations rapidly should have positive effects on producers knowledge.

Amongst collectors, packagers and distributors of information the most adversely effected will be the collectors of information and those whose work functions involve the organisation of information into various forms. To the extent that decisions will need to be made on forms in which information is to be organised for different purposes – work functions commonly performed by research assistants, administrative assistants, editors, government, business and institutional bureaucrats – those performing such decisions will not be affected adversely in relation to their work functions, but their numbers may be effected adversely because of easy access to information and the capacity of computers to convert that information into any form almost instantaneously.

The work functions of many applicators of knowledge will change, and that will probably effect negatively employment in the relevant occupations: when search and selection of legal precedents is carried out efficiently and rapidly by computers, a substantial part of the lawyers work functions is eliminated; and when all kinds of standard contracts are easily accessible from computer peripherals, the relevant role of the lawyer is reduced further. Similarly, when computers and computer peripherals measure and analyse all vital signs, provide a diagnosis and suggest an appropriate medication, the work-functions of the physician are reduced to the examination and verification of the work performed by the computer. The role of the physician may remain vital, but the range of work functions may decrease significantly.

Many service occupants perform their work functions out of office settings of all kinds. The application of microelectronic processes to all or most office functions will impact severely on office employment. The office is largely an information processing centre. Any technology which will speed-up the processing of information will impact on employment in the office. When information is deposited into a computer and is accessed to a video-screen, examined, amended, supplemented, transformed into configurations, and transferred to paper, scores of manual office activities are eliminated. The capacity of computers and word processors to store information dispenses with filing and routine clerical activities; the capacity to access information on the video-screen dispenses with activities related to searches of written information, the placing of that information on paper, and the delivery of the paper from office to office; and the capacity to transform the information into various configurations and transfer it to paper dispenses with certain clerical and typing activities. There are, of course, scores of other clerical and secretarial activities that are performed in the average office, and aside from clerical functions specifically related to the operation of computer-systems, such as, data entry and data control, we do not really know the nature of work activities that will emerge in operations dominated by microelectronic instruments and processes. Nevertheless, it can be expected with a reasonable degree of certainty that many of the work-functions performed by people in offices today will not be performed by people within the next 25 years. This does not mean that the people who perform such work-functions today will have no work-functions to perform and will thereby become unemployed. It only means that they will perform some other functions.

Occupations Employed in Computer Systems

The introduction of computer technology created a wide range of work-functions, occupations and employments: information systems managers, business systems managers, system development specialists, systems maintenance and control specialists, data base administration activities, management science specialists, computer services specialists, system analysts, programmers, computer operators, data control clerks, data entry operators, and scores of other occupations and employments related to the development, operation and maintenance of systems.

Generally, the number and occupational mix of employees associated with the operation of individual computer and computer-related systems tend to vary with the type of system in operation, the nature of activity in which the system is put, and whether the organisation employing the system develops in-house software or purchases packaged programmes (Table 7.1): managerial/administrative occupations

TABLE 7.1 *Percentage breakdown of data processing employment by occupation in selected industries, 1980*

	Primary	*Construction*	*Manufacturing*	*Transportation*	*Public utility*	*Communication*	*Distribution*	*Financial*
Manager/administrative	17.4	18.7	12.5	13.3	13.8	12.7	16.1	11.7
Systems analysts	14.6	6.2	11.0	10.5	15.5	11.6	6.8	14.5
Programmers	21.7	20.6	17.0	26.0	28.8	20.0	16.1	17.0
Professional specialists (engineers, operations research specialists)	0.6	—	2.2	0.5	2.3	1.3	0.3	0.3
Subtotal: managerial & professional	54.3	45.5	42.7	50.3	60.4	45.6	39.3	43.5
Computer & equipment operators	15.7	20.6	15.5	14.5	15.5	19.6	19.0	15.6
Data control clerks	4.8	5.7	5.8	4.3	5.2	6.2	6.7	6.8
Data entry clerks	24.7	28.2	25.3	26.4	18.6	25.9	34.6	32.7
Other	0.4	—	10.7	4.6	0.6	2.8	0.4	1.5
Total	99.9	100.0	100.0	100.1	100.0	100.1	100.0	100.1

SOURCE Compiled from various publications.

account for 12 to 19 per cent of total system employment; systems analysts account for 6 to 16 per cent; programmers make up 16 to 29 per cent; computer equipment operators account for 15 to 21 per cent; data entry clerks represent 19 to 35 per cent; and data control clerks 4 to 7 per cent. The occupational distribution in public utilities is of particular interest since it signals perhaps the things to come. Public utilities generally are on the forefront of automated electronic systems. The occupational composition of their employment may well be a model of the nature of composition we should expect generally when similar integrated systems are introduced in other establishments. Should such be the case, we must expect demand for programmers and systems analysts to increase and demand for data entry clerks to fall. This will mean further declines in demand for occupations requiring relatively low levels of education and skills.

The extent to which low-level occupations disappear as computer and communications systems become increasingly integrated, and the extent to which middle and high level occupations predominate in the occupational composition of employment, is evidenced in Table 7.2. It contains the divisional organisation of an Information Systems Department, the occupations employed in it, and the work functions associated with each occupational classification.

The divisional distribution provides perhaps an indication of the nature of activities that are involved in a comprehensive information system, and the occupational groups that are involved within individual activity areas. Thus, the *Information Systems Division* is involved in the determination of the information requirements of the organisation, and the development, implementation and maintenance of systems for the attainment of the determined requirements. These are high level activities, and that is reflected in the occupational composition of personnel involved in them: the entire complement is constituted of managers and professionals. *The Information Facilities Division* is the operational division: it directs planning and technical support of computer and telecommunications facilities, provides computer services, and is generally responsible for the maintenance of an operational infrastructure which will fulfill the organisation's requirements. The Division's manpower complement reflects an operational system: computer operators, data entry control clerks, data entry operators – predominantly non-professional occupational groups.

Those are the two main divisions. There are then the *Data Base Administration Division*, involved in data base design, problem solving, access control, and training programme coordination; *the Management*

TABLE 7.2 *Information resources department of a food processor/wholesaler/distributor*

Division	*Manpower*	*Functions*
Information resources		
	Director	
Financial control	Analyst	coordinates and controls financial activities in the information resources department.
Administrative support	Administrative secretary	Provides administrative support to management and professionals in the information resources department.
	Secretary	
Information system	Manager	Directs the planning and implementation of management information systems.
Business systems	Managers	Determine systems requirements of the organisation.
Systems development	Manager	Design, implement and assess business information systems.
	Project managers	
	Analysts	
	Programmers	
Systems maintenance and control	Manager	Provide maintenance support and quality control on new and operating systems.
	Coordinators	
	Analysts	
Information Facilities	Manager	Directs planning and technical support of computer and telecommuncations facilities.
	Secretary	
Computer services	Manager	
	Supervisor	
	Operations analysts	Provide computer services and technical support for computer facilities.
	Planners	
	Computer operators	
	Data control clerks	
	Data entry operators	

Technical services and support	Manager Analysts	Control activities relating to the operating system and provide software package support and maintenance.
Telecommunications	Manager Console attendant	Plans, monitors and controls telecommunications.
Facilities planning and control	Manager	Plans the acquisition of computer hardware and telecommunications equipment.
Date base administration	Manager Analysts	Data definition, standards and access authority.
Technology	Specialist Analyst	Senior consultation for problem solving.
Education	Coordinator	Coordinates training programmes.
Management science	Manager Specialists Analyst	Mathematical and Statistical Modelling and Operations Research.
Record management	Manager Technician	Plans, designs and administers records and forms.
	Administrators Analysts	Coordinate information retrieval, security and computer output on microforms and systems. Produce policy and procedure manuals.
Office Systems	Manager Analyst	Plan and develop automated office systems.
	W. P. operators	Provide text editing, TWX, Telex and voice communications services.

Sciences Division, which is involved in mathematical and statistical modelling and operations research; *the Records Management Division*, involved in the design of forms, policy and procedure manuals, and the coordination of information retrieval and security; and the *Office Systems Division*, involved in planning and development of automated office systems, and in secretarial (text editing, TWX, telex) services.

The occupational distribution of the manpower complement reflects the specialised nature of computer system activities: almost three-quarters are managers, analysts and programmers. The entire department is serviced by only three secretaries, one of whom is the department's administrative secretary, who also employs one of the other two secretaries. But, there are word processing operators, data control clerks, data entry operators, and a console attendant, all of whom are former clerks and secretaries. Hence, what we are witnessing is an adjustment to technological change that is not much different from the adjustments that have been recorded through history. Work functions change and with the change in work functions job titles, job classifications and job descriptions will change. Some secretaries will become 'assistants', some will become 'word processing operators', some will become 'specialists', and others 'advisors', 'counsellors', and so on. It is not possible to determine at present the nature of occupational concentrations that will emerge from the on-going changes in computer and telecommunications technology. The electronic infrastructure is still in the very early phase of development. What will ultimately emerge, and what manpower complements and occupational groupings will be required for its efficient functioning, is anybody's guess. But, in the foreseeable future, as systems expand and integrate, the most likely occupational structure will evolve in the pattern indicated above, namely, increasing demand for analysts, specialists in various aspects of system design and operations, and software specialists, and decreasing demand for conventional clerical occupations.

This has important implications for the employment of women. Since women occupy most of the non-professional positions, such as data control clerks, data-entry operators, word-processing operators, and computer operators, it can be concluded that women continue to predominate in low-level employment positions – a natural outcome of the failure of women to enter into programmes which produce computer and systems-related specialists. This is a failure and an opportunity. Considering the general shortage of systems analysts and programmers, the anticipated continuing increase in demand for them, and the fact that most senior positions in systems departments are occupied by such specialists and other persons knowledgeable in computer systems, an opportunity is presented for a significant change in the male and female composition of high-level occupational groups. Although we cannot expect clerks to become analysts, we can fully expect decreasing numbers of women to become clerks and increasing numbers to become analysts. It is a matter of time.

Concluding Remarks

The information contained in this section provides a reasonably good indication of the nature of occupational specialisations and occupational complements that are required for the operation of computer and computer-related systems. Generally, the manpower mix appears to be 75 per cent managerial, professional, and technical and 25 per cent non-professional. This is significantly different from the present composition of the labour force, in which the professional, managerial and technical occupational group represents only about 25 per cent of the total. Most changes in the number and nature of activities introduced to-date, as a result of the implementation of computer systems, are generally regarded as the first step, the initial phase, of a continuously changing infrastructure. No one, not even the most knowledgeable, could say what level of employment and occupational mix will emerge when full integration of electronic systems is attained.

The evidence from integrated systems suggests three significant developments: *One is* a tendency for employments to increase only minimally in response to very substantial increases in the physical size and operations of a system. Once a computer infrastructure is in place and the requisite manpower complement is employed on it, the system can be expanded into an extensive network with only minimal increments in manpower. *The second* development is the change in occupational mix. While total employment may remain relatively stable as a system expands, its composition undergoes significant changes: a notable shift takes place towards higher level professional and managerial/administrative classifications. *The third* development is the decrease of employment in low level operational activities, such as data entry. A switch from batch to interactive systems, for example, will facilitate VDT data entry directly from offices, thereby eliminating the need for the 'assembly line' operational activities performed by keypunch operators. This is a common outcome of the introduction of on-line systems: the input process becomes part of other clerical activities performed within the office.

Occupational Trends

Although work functions are expected to change significantly over the next 25 years, which will cause significant changes to individual occupations and within occupational groups, the proportions of so-called 'white-collar' and 'blue-collar' occupations are not likely to change substantially. Perhaps two or three percentages in the direction of the white-collar group will take place as more and more skilled and semi-skilled production-process jobs are eliminated, and as some skilled production-process workers become information process assistants and consultants. But, no greater shifts are expected.[2]

Service sector occupations are projected to continue to grow faster than total employment: occupations in which employment grew faster than the average rate of employment growth over the past two decades, such as clerical occupations and occupations providing services of all kinds, will continue to grow faster than the average of total employment; the rate of growth in clerical and other office occupations will be effected negatively by the increasing introduction of electronic capital instruments in the office, but over the next two decades the overall effect is expected to be nothing more than a decrease in the rate of increase to slightly more than the average rate of incrase in total employment, instead of substantially more as would have been the case in the absence of such instruments; occupations providing services of all kinds to individuals, families, business, and institutions are expected to continue the fast growth recorded over the past two decades, which has been considerably faster than the average rate of growth in total employment; professional and technical occupations are projected to grow faster than average employment, with the fastest rate in occupations related specifically to all aspects of information processing.

Goods-producing sector blue-collar occupations are projected to continue the gradual decline experienced heretofore: most skilled production-process occupations are expected to be negatively effected by the increasing introduction of electronic instruments; and employment in assembly line occupations is expected to decrease substantially.

Employment in activities requiring professional and technical knowledge will continue to increase rapidly. Microelectronic technology will eliminate routine, time-consuming functions and thereby enable professional practitioners to devote more time to higher level functions. We know, for example, that the majority of patients visiting doctors' offices suffer psychosomatic illnesses, and that they will be helped more by discussion about what does not pain them physically than by what does. Therefore, to the extent that microelectronic technology will speed-up physical examinations and diagnoses, the physician will have more time for the discussion of personal problems that predispose individuals to illness. The same applies, of course, to nurses. When microelectronic technology will enable them to voice-record directly into the computer all information about their patients, the time they now allocate to charting will be available for talking with patients. And patients need to talk. They are concerned about their illnesses; they are concerned about the outcome of the treatments they are given; they want to know about possible alternatives to what is being suggested; they are concerned about their families; their jobs; and so on. Other professional and technical workers, such as engineers, scientists, accountants, and technicians of all kinds have benefitted substantially from electronic advancements to-date, and will likely benefit even more from future innovations. The transfer of number crunching to computers has vacated a very substantial amount of time for other work-functions.

Projected trends in occupational groups do not, of course, mean that all occupations that make up each group will experience the trend rate of change: some will change faster than the trend rate of the group and some slower. For example, the *professional and technical group of occupations* (15.9 per cent of total employment in the US in 1978) is constituted of teachers, medical professionals, all kinds of health and welfare related professionals and paraprofessionals, engineers, accountants, dentists, architects, economists and statisticians, and scores of other social, scientific and technical professional and paraprofessional occupations. Employment in the group is expected to continue to increase at a faster rate than the average for all occupations.[3] But within the group rates will vary: employment in medical, health and welfare occupations generally is expected to increase faster than the average, while employment in teaching occupations is expected to increase slower than the average; employment of computer systems analysts is projected to increase about five times faster than the average for all occupations, while employment of dental-hygienists, physical therapists, child care attendants and veterinarians, for example, is projected to increase about two-and-one-half times faster than the average for all occupations. Employment of *sales workers* (6.6 per cent of total employment in 1978), half of whom are in retail trade and the remainder in manufacturing, finance, insurance and real estate is projected to increase faster than the average for all occupations; and so is the employment of *clerical workers* (18.3 per cent of total employment in 1978), about 20 per cent of whom are secretaries and typists, and the remainder general office workers, cashiers, bookkeepers, and stock clerks. It is recognised that office automation will enable clerical personnel to produce more within given periods of time, and will eliminate some of their work functions, which will cause changes in the skill requirements of some occupations, but 'continued increases in the demand for new workers are anticipated in most occupations'.[4]

Employment in the *craft and kindred workers* group of occupations (12 per cent of total employment in 1978) is projected to increase slightly faster than the average for all occupations. But, significant variations are expected within the group: construction trades are expected to increase rapidly; and so are metalworking crafts; data processing machine mechanics are expected to grow very fast (about seven or eight times faster than the rate for all occupations), while the employment of railway car repair mechanics is expected to decrease; office machine and cash register service occupations are projected to grow at about three times the rate for all occupations, while employment of printing trades is expected to fall.

Employment in the '*operatives*' group of occupations (14.6 per cent of total employment in 1978) is projected to increase slower than the average for all occupations. The group is constituted of assemblers, machine and tool operators, welders, transport equipment operators (truck and bus drivers), and inspectors in manufacturing. Here, too, variations can be expected: demand for machine and tool operators will increase faster than the average, while employment of welders will decrease. Robots already perform most of the welding work in automobile manufacturing, and over time will likely take over that work function from welders in most large establishments.

Demand for *service workers* (13.6 per cent of total employment in 1978), is expected to increase faster than any other occupational group. Included in this category are food service occupations, health service occupations, such as nurses' aides, medical assistants, and generally service workers in hospitals and nursing homes, police officers and other security personnel, firefighters and other protective service workers and welfare service workers, building and house cleaning workers, outside municipal service workers, and many others. But, as with the other occupational groups, employment in some of these will increase faster than in others. For example, it is expected that the rate of increase for health and welfare service workers will be very fast, the rate for police and other law enforcement and security personnel will not be as fast, because of the increasing deployment of sophisticated electronic monitoring devices in homes and business establishments, and the rate for barbers, hairdressers and cosmetologists will be only moderate.

Amongst the other occupational groups, employment in the *farmers and farm workers* groups is expected to continue its decline, while employment in the *private household workers* group may increase, as increasing numbers of women enter into paid employment outside the home. There are indications that the strong demand for household services will result in the establishment of domestic service enterprises. Such a development may remove a number of the factors responsible for the decline of employment in domestic service, namely, low productivity, low pay, and low social status. When a service is contracted and provided through an enterprise, its nature is specified precisely, eliminating the possibility of being asked to do work of a kind one does not wish to do, and it removes the stigma associated with domestic

TABLE 7.3 *Projections of the 20 most rapidly growing occupations in the USA*

Occupation	*% change 1978–90*	
	Low trend	*High trend*
Data processing machine mechanics	147.6	173.0
Para-legal personnel	132.4	165.7
Computer systems analysts	107.8	123.0
Computer operators	87.9	100.7
Office machine & cash register services	80.8	96.2
Computer programmers	73.6	86.9
Aero astronotic engineers	70.4	80.9
Food preparation and service work	68.8	77.1
in fast food establishments	66.6	85.6
Employment interviewers	64.5	87.8
Tax preparers	60.3	63.1
Correction officials and jailers	60.2	70.2
Architects	57.9	61.4
Dental hygienists	57.6	66.5
Physical therapists	57.5	61.0
Dental assistants	57.3	65.6
Peripheral EDP equipment operators	56.3	67.9
Child care attendants	56.1	70.3
Travel agents	55.6	65.6
Nurses' aides & orderlies	54.6	65.4

SOURCE Max L. Carey, 'Occupational Employment Growth Through 1990', *Monthly Labor Review*, 104 (Aug. 1981) p. 48.

service. The service is deemed to be rendered to the enterprise, not to a specific household.

The occupational groups that are expected to record the fastest rates of employment growth to 1990 in the US are given in Table 7.3. The impact of microelectronic instruments and processes is evident: with only one exception, the fastest rates by far are expected to be in occupations involved directly with the operation and maintenance of computer systems. The employment of data processing machine mechanics is expected to grow seven to eight times faster than the average for all occupations; computer systems analysts five to six times faster; and computer programmers three to four times faster.

Projections of individual occupations, like projections of occupational groups, relate to an average for the occupation. Many occupations, like occupational groups, are constituted of a multitude of occupational classifications, each classification performing different work functions. Demand for each is influenced by different market forces. For example, the overall demand for teachers may be projected to fall, remain unchanged or increase at a slower rate than the average for all occupations. But, all teachers are not teaching the same subjects and all subjects are not equally effected by technological and other changes. Some of the knowledge that is being taught may well become redundant as a result of the introduction of electronic instruments and processes, and some may be expanded as a result. Teachers involved in instruction in the use of computers will be in increasing demand, while teachers teaching some of the vocational and technical subjects effected adversely by microelectronic technology will face decreasing demand for their services. Similarly, although the demand for engineers may be projected at a rate higher than the rate for all occupations, all engineering specialisations will not necessarily experience the higher rate: electronics engineers will probably experience a very high rate, but civil engineers will probably have a much lower rate; typists will probably experience a much lower rate than secretaries; and sales workers in retail trade will probably experience a higher rate than sales workers in finance, insurance and real estate.

Effect on Occupational Skills

Do advances in technology need an increasingly more educated and skilled labour force or do they lower educational and skill requirements? It is generally assumed that:[5]

1 Semi-automatic and automatic machinery and equipment require higher levels of skill and education than does conventional machinery.
2 Semi-automatic and automatic machinery and instruments require a higher degree of work specialisation for maintenance.
3 The design, production and installation of automatic machinery requires more specialised engineers and technicians than does conventional machinery.
4 The change from conventional to automatic machinery is so radical and so fundamental as to make it either very difficult or impossible for workers to shift from the one process to the other.
5 Even where the average worker is not deficient in skill relative to the skill requirements of the automatic machines, it is alleged that he feels instinctively inadequately prepared for the work environment of the automatic process.[6].

It is this sort of reasoning that is at the foundation of the prevailing view that high level technology will require high levels of education and skills. But, generally accepted expectations and beliefs do not appear to find support in the reality of work processes. James R. Bright writes:

> I was startled to find that the upgrading effect had not occurred to anywhere near the extent that is often assumed. . . . I found frequent instances in which management's stated belief that automation had required a higher caliber of work force skill was refuted when the facts were explored.[7]

This does not mean that automation does not create new skills and does not require educational and skill upgrading. It means rather that on the average the extent to which skill upgrading is required as a result appears to have been exaggerated. Indeed, Bright concluded: ' . . . automated machinery tends to require less operator skill after certain levels of mechanisation are achieved. . . . automation does not inevitably mean lack of opportunity for the unskilled worker'.[8] This is confirmed by the findings of Jaffe and Froomkin in relation to highly mechanised processes. They write: 'Our broad-based statistical findings confirm . . . that the workers generally needed no additional schooling to fill a job which became highly mechanised.'[9]

But there is a question which does not appear to have been asked: is it possible that educational and skill *requirements* have increased, but were accommodated imperceptibly by workers who have had higher educational and skill qualifications than what was required of them for the performance of the work functions assigned to them in the displaced processes. It is generally recognised that in advanced industrial economies the levels of education possessed by labour forces are, on the average, higher than what is required at any given period. Given such an excess in qualifications relative to requirements, the possibility exists of substitutions amongst levels of education, knowledge and skills. Industries have the opportunity to choose those sets of educational and skill qualifications which suit them best. Perhaps this is the reason for the lack of concern about educational and skill qualifications. On the average, qualifications have been higher than the requirements of instruments and processes. The educational and skill capacity of workers to accommodate changes that require more education and higher skill may well convey the impression that upgrading does not take place.

Furthermore, the conclusions reached by the investigators relate largely to formal education only; account is not taken of the supplementary and complementary education provided in the work place. An investigation by the author found a considerable amount of such education.[10] Respondents wrote:

> our organisation is more or less geared to technological change, . . . our people average a technical upgrading course every six to nine months.
>
> . . . to provide the necessary changes in skills to cope with the technological change, we not only do a large amount of on-the-job training but we operate three separate training schools.
>
> . . . lack of qualified personnel is seldom a delaying factor because through long experience we have learned to make the retraining and development of the personnel required an integral part of the planning of the technological change.
>
> . . . the gradual and deliberate upgrading of our employees' skills through "on-the-job" and "in-house" training is sufficient to meet the demands of these changes.
>
> . . . we have never been aware of the technological change being a major problem. We have always had on-going in-plant trade development programs as a result of attrition and normal upgrading.
>
> . . . we have found that succeeding technological changes have tended to reduce the number of jobs requiring the least education and skill. . . . as processes and controls and equipment are automated the remaining positions require a higher degree of comprehension, skill and education. As a result we have had to organise training, for

employees who would be taking new duties, to a greater degree than in past years.
. . . certainly changes do require on occasion new skills and it is our general practice to provide this training ourselves.

We did not seek information on the formal educational attainment of the workers involved. But, many respondents made specific reference to the higher levels of education of employees today than five or ten years ago, having facilitated the introduction of more comprehensive, and higher level, 'in-house' training programmes. Which suggests that had levels of formal education not been higher, 'on-the-job' and 'in-house' programmes may not have been at the levels of technical sophistication required for the new technology.

Education-Technology: Cause and Effect

Commonly, the issue of the relationship between technological change and employment, and technological change, education, skills and the occupational composition of the labour force are examined from the standpoint of technological changes being the cause and changes in the other variables being the effect. The issue of the effect on technological changes – contemplated or implemented – of existing levels of education, skills, and the occupational composition of the labour force is not as frequently examined. For example, are there delays in the implementation of technological changes because of deficiencies in education and skills? Is there evidence of sub-optimal utilisation of technological changes because of an inadequately prepared labour force?

We know that there has been a gap between inventions and their development and application in production processes; and we know also that the gap has been narrowing in recent times. Lynn identifies two initial periods in the development of technology:[11]

1 'A period . . . when little or nothing of a concrete nature occurs because although technical feasibility has been established, a number of missing elements must be supplied before the commercial potential becomes evident.' He labels this the 'Incubation Period'.
2 'Once the commercial potential has been recognised, a period of commercial development ensues when a directed effort is made to convert the basic technology into a technically and economically feasible product or process.' He labels this period the 'Commercial Development Period'.

TABLE 7.4 *Rate of development for selected technological innovations*

Technological innovations	*Start of commerical develop-ment*	*Lapsed time (years)* Incuba-tion period	Commercial develop-ment	Total develop-ment
Aluminium	1886	31	6	37
Motor vehicle transportation	1891	23	4	27
Air transportation	1903	6	8	14
Synthetic resins	1907	49	3	52
Radio broadcasting	1913	17	9	26
Electronic vacuum tubes	1914	7	6	13
Frozen goods	1916	74	9	83
Vitamins	1926	13	11	24
Synthetic rubber	1929	20	11	31
Television broadcasting	1933	22	12	34
Synthetic fibres	1936	6	3	9
Titanium	1936	26	14	40
Antibiotics	1939	11	1	12
Electronic computers	1944	15	6	21
Semiconductors	1948	7	3	10
Numerical control	1948	18	7	25
Synthetic leather	1950	12	14	26
Nuclear power generation	1954	11	3	14
Freeze-dried foods	1955	4	6	10
Integrated circuits	1958	2	3	5
Average		19	7	26

SOURCE Frank Lynn, *Ibid*, p. 39; see footnote 11, chapter 7.

Table 7.4 shows the incubation and commercial development periods of various innovations and demonstrates the extent to which the gap has tended to narrow in recent times.

It is quite appropriate to pose the question, to what extent, if any, is the invention-implementation gap related to the educational attainment of the labour force? Is it possible that the narrowing temporal gap of recent times is related to the fact that levels of education have been generally rising?

A. J. Jaffe and J. Froomkin write:

> An analysis of changes in the educational attainment of workers by growth in level of output per worker reveals that the speed of technological change has little, if anything to do with educational

> attainment . . . even in those industries which apparently were undergoing the most rapid technological changes (as measured by changes in output per worker), one half to three-quarters of the manual workers had less than high school education. These data clearly prove that modern advancing technology does not necessarily require workers to have more formal schooling.[12]

The authors state that their observations apply equally to the educational attainment of nonprofessional white-collar workers.[13]

These findings are in general agreement with those of Bright[14] and Fine,[15] who concluded that workers generally did not need additional schooling to fill jobs in highly mechanised processes. Which, by implication, means also that the implementation of highly mechanised processes was not impeded by the level of schooling of the labour force. In some instances periods of training for the highly mechanised processes tended to be a little longer than for previous changes in equipment, but these were a matter of a few weeks on the job.

In our investigation[16] we found that 76 per cent of responding industries encountered no manpower difficulties in the implementation of technological changes. Familiarisation with the new technology was naturally necessary, and it involved varying periods of orientation; but the orientation process was no different in substance than that to which newly hired workers are subjected.

The 24 per cent of responding industries who reported delays in the implementation and/or in the optimum utilisation of new technology gave as the major cause 'inadequate supply of specialised manpower'. Scarcity of systems analysts, computer programmers, mechanics, implementation officers, electronics technicians, caused postponements in the implementation of planned technological changes in some instances, and delays in capacity utilisation in other. But, there was no indication in the responses that the available manpower could not cope with the new technology. On the contrary, the responses provide a basis for the general conclusion that the level of general and technical education possessed by the labour force is, on the average, higher than what is currently required for the implementation and optimal utilisation of modern industrial and commercial production processes.

This may, of course, be the reason for not encountering difficulties in the implementation and efficient utilisation of new technology: in anticipation of advances in science and technology, academic institutions have offered appropriate educational programmes, and the labour force became better equipped for what was to come.[17]

Lynn makes no reference to education as a possible factor in the innovation-development gap. He attributes the gap instead to three other factors: (1) the nature of the application – whether for the consumer market or for the industrial market – apparently, consumer market innovations have had a narrower gap than industrial market innovations; (2) the source of development funds – whether private or public. Apparently the financing of development by governments in recent times has been an important factor in the narrowing of the gap, particularly so in relation to innovations that have implications for defence and space exploration; (3) Patent protection. The rationale here is that when patents are held by the public authority and development of the innovations is open to competition, faster development and application can be expected than when patents are privately held.

Edwin Mansfield, a leading authority on the economics of technological change, also fails to make any reference to the effect of education and skills on technological change.[18] He has examined the relationship between the size of firms and the development of innovations; the relationship between the application of innovations and the relative increase in the firm's economic advantage; the uncertainty associated with the development of innovations; the financial commitments required in attempting development; and the potential profitability of investment in research and development; but not the relationship between the level of schooling of the labour force and the development of innovations.

In summary, the evidence appears to suggest that technological innovations and their application in *advanced industrial economies* have not been held back by the educational and technical preparation of the labour force. Although without doubt the inventive and developmental activity in such economies is related somewhat to the level of education and technical competence of the labour force, there is no evidence of any *direct* relationship between the rate of technological change and the educational level of the labour force.[19]

To the extent that there exists a relationship between levels of education, innovation and technological development, it is likely to be found in connection with R & D activity. If a close relationship were established between R & D activity and technological change, and there is a relationship between R & D activity and employment of high level manpower, then a relationship can be deduced between technological change and the educational level of the labour force.

The foregoing relates, of course, to the labour forces of developed, industrialised economies, and it is in the context of the technological structure of such economies. It does not apply to countries which are not technologically advanced.

This conclusion will be found disturbing by some; common observations appear to suggest otherwise. We noted, for example, that computer related occupations, such as programmers, required relatively high educational qualifications in the early phases of development and operation of computer systems, but as knowledge of the technology increased, the educational qualifications for its operation appear to have decreased. Similar outcomes are suggested by a superficial examination of many areas of activity in which microelectronic instruments and processes have been applied: aircraft takeoff, land and fly on computer-controlled instruments, which reduce significantly the range of work-functions required of pilots, navigators and other crew members; many of the high level work-functions that laboratory technicians used to perform are now performed by automated computer processes; and the writing function has virtually disappeared from all computerised clerical activities.

The deskilling of some occupations is, of course, a well known historical reality of technological change; and it is similarly well known that advances in knowledge render some knowledge redundant. But, the overall effect of the technology appears to be upgrading. The occupational distribution of employees associated with the operation of computers and computer-related systems is generally of higher skill and education than the occupational complement of other technologies in history. No other technology has required as high and as varied occupational qualifications for its operation: there is almost no comparison between the operatives of electromechanical systems, or the clerks of a manual office system, and the various levels of analysts, programmers, mathematical and statistical specialists, operators and data entry and data control personnel required for the operation of computer systems.

From the Reality of Yesterday to Tomorrow

Occupational knowledge is rendered redundant by two developments: by the advance in knowledge, and by the transference of knowledge from humans into equipment, materials and processes. The critical issue for occupations and employment tomorrow is this: how much human knowledge can be embodied into microelectronic instruments and processes, and to what extent the instruments and processes will use that knowledge in production activities without human intervention. In other words, how much human knowledge and intelligence will be transferred to computers and other microelectronic instruments and processes, and what will the instruments and processes be able to do with that knowledge and intelligence. Will they be limited in their operational activities to the knowledge and intelligence that is transferred to them, or will they have the capacity to use that knowledge and intelligence to create knowledge? To the extent that they are limited to what they are instructed by human producers of software, human direction and control will be maintained; but, to the extent that they use the knowledge to create knowledge, and thereby become self-directive in productive activities, human intervention will be reduced significantly. The fundamental issue is whether their operational activities will be limited to the transferred intelligence, or whether they will have the capacity to use the knowledge and intelligence embodied into them to become self-directive. To the extent that they become self-directive, their activities will effectively be governed by a combination of *transferred intelligence* and *artificial intelligence*.

Whether limited in the range of their operational activities to the knowledge and intelligence transferred to them, or expanded to other activities as well through the application of artificial intelligence, the impact on human operational activities can be expected to be considerable. In activities to which microelectronic technology can be applied effectively, the transfer of occupational knowledge to microelectronic instruments and processes will render the corresponding human occupational knowledge redundant; and the transfer of intelligence to microelectronic instruments and processes will render inferior all those of lesser intelligence. This has important implications for the adjustment process: skill redundancy can be overcome through retraining in occupational activities not transferred to instruments and processes; we have not had equal experience with inferior intelligence. Is it possible to raise the level of intelligence of people above the level embodied in instruments and processes?

It is not our intention to extend this discussion into the realm of science fiction. But, the possibility does exist that microelectronic instruments and processes will be provided with the knowledge and capacity to perform a wide range of activities requiring relatively high levels of intelligence. Such a development will place at a competitive disadvantage increasing proportions of the population. The critical question in relation to employment is not *whether* microelectronic instruments and processes will have the capacity to perform activities that require relatively high levels of knowledge and intelligence, but rather *the range* of activities to which microelectronic instruments and processes will be applied. The wider the range of activities, the greater will be the threat to employment. Mechanical instruments and processes have had relatively limited negative effects on employment because of the limited range of activities to which they were applied. The work activities in which most of the people were engaged could not have been performed by mechanical instruments. The possibility is now presented that microelectronic instruments and processes will be applied to most activities in which people engage. Furthermore, the level of skill knowledge embodied in microelectronic instruments is considerably greater than what was embodied in mechanical instruments, and in addition, microelectronic instruments have been endowed with decision-making powers. They can become formidable competitors in the work place, at all levels of work activity.

On the other hand, there are some positive elements in this: the transfer to microelectronic instruments and processes of routine and cumbersome functions, will vacate brain power for higher level functions. Unburdened by information that no longer has to be remembered, and uncluttered by functions that no longer have to be performed, people will allocate more thought to higher-level functions, and to functions which cannot be readily assumed by electronic instruments. The personal, the social, the aesthetic, the cultural are such functions. Educational and training processes concerned with occupations that render services to people as individuals, as members of families and as members of society, will shift their attention more and more to these aspects of human existence.

8 Employment Effects: the Establishment and the Economy

Introduction

This is perhaps a wrong time to be writing on employment implications of a new technology. Lack of economic growth has limited the macroeconomic offsets to structural and technological changes, and unemployment created deliberately by public policy distorts the reality of economic processes and their effects. Under normal economic conditions the technologically displaced workers from activity X will be picked up, with or without retraining, for employment in activity Y. If there is no expansion in activity Y, the worker will not be picked up. Which suggests that the problem is not with activity X, but rather with activity Y. Although some would assert that if activity Y is in a state of stagnation, as the economy at large has been, then activity X should not be permitted to displace the worker at this time. It should postpone the technological change until better conditions prevail.

Nevertheless, the issue is that at any point of time we have technological unemployment, structural unemployment, seasonal unemployment, frictional unemployment, so-called cyclical unemployment, and induced unemployment. When all of these converge, as they have currently, it is hardly an appropriate time to measure effectively and argue convincingly the case for accelerated technological change. Rational arguments founded on the reality of growth, adjustment, and employment creation are rejected as being removed from the actual reality of the process where the substitution takes place. The emphasis is on the reality of the displaced clerical worker, not on the fact that the clerical worker would have been placed elsewhere into employment if there were economic expansion. And the emphasis assumes hysterical proportions when the experience of the displaced clerical worker is extrapolated to all clerical workers, as an inevitable consequence of the new technological processes.

The debate about the employment effects of microelectronic technology is not a debate about structural employment effects or technological employment effects. It is rather a debate about effects on employment generally. No one would deny the proposition that changes in industry structure initiated or facilitated by microelectronic technology will result in some structural unemployment. Some industries, processes and activities will inevitably decline, just as many have declined as a result of the advent of other technologies, products and processes in the past. Equally, no one would deny the proposition that the new knowledge imbedded in microelectronic technology will render redundant some existing knowledge, which means the skills of some people will become redundant. But given economic growth and general expansion in employment, these kinds of unemployment have been corrected in the past through retraining and mobility from declining industries and employments to expanding industries and employments. The concern now is that computers, microprocessors and telecommunications technology will enable expanding industries to increase their outputs manyfold without the employment of additional labour. In which case, neither the structurally and technologically unemployed, nor the projected increase in the labour force will be accommodated in alternative employments.[1]

When examining the effects of technology *on employment generally*, account must be taken of the effects on *six levels of employment*: *the first level* is that associated with the production of the technology – the design, testing, financing, manufacture, distribution and demonstration of the technology – as well as the employments associated with processes supplying the technology producer with materials and services. *The second level* of employment effect is that associated with the application of the technology – the employment positions that are eliminated, and the employment positions that are created at the operational level. The secretary, the typist, the filing clerk, the administrative assistant, the word processor operator, the computer operator, the programmer, the repair and maintenance technician. *The third level* is the employment associated with the management of the technology infrastructure and the resultant output – professional and administrative personnel, sales personnel, finance, planning, and such other. *The fourth level* is the employment at processes external to the firm, but associated with the firm's output – processes preceding the process of the firm, such as suppliers of materials and services, and processes following the process of the firm, such as transportation, distribution, storage and promotion. *The fifth level* is a general form of employment associated with the provision of transportation services, financial services, insurance, real estate services, municipal and other public services to all enterprises. *The sixth and final level* is the employment that is derived from the expenditure of the incomes earned by the factors of production participating in the multitude of processes. Any technology or varying technologies applied at any one of the first five levels may result in negative employment at that level. The critical question is what happens in the other levels; what is the net effect, on the aggregate. That is, what happens to the number of the employment multiplier.

Most pronouncements regarding the employment effects of microelectronic technology relate to only the second level of employment – the level at which the technology is applied – and are limited to the immediate effect. No account is taken of effects at the other levels, and no consideration is given to the employment effect of an increase in output. Yet, the second level employment effect will be affected not only by the direct impact of the technology but also by the rate of increase in demand and output relative to the rate of increase in productivity. Even a tenfold increase in productivity may not affect employment negatively if demand and output were to increase tenfold – not an inconceivable development in the longer run, even though problematical over the short run.

Employment in individual industries, occupations and employments can, of course, be affected negatively; the labour intensity of production processes can be expected to decrease; and the pervasiveness of microelectronic technology can be expected to reduce the number of the employment multiplier. The net result could be a decrease in demand for labour. But, this will not be an unusual occurrence. The application of labour to production processes has been decreasing throughout history: children are no longer employed in the numbers in which they were employed; the proportion of those 65 years of age and over who remain in full-time and part-time employment has fallen to less than 20 per cent of their number; and the actual hours of work of the employed have fallen to an average of about six per day. Historically, there have been *three unemployment offsets* to technology-induced decreases in labour intensity of production processes: (1) the decrease in hours of work; (2) increase in demand for goods and services generally; and (3) the production of a wide range of new goods and services. There is no reason not to expect the continuing operation of these three offsets.

Reasons for Concern

Concerns about negative employment effects of microelectronics are founded on four preconceptions: *one is that the quantities of goods and services to be produced are fixed.* Therefore, any technology which makes it possible to produce a larger quantity of goods and services per unit of work time will make it possible to produce the fixed quantity of goods and services with fewer workers. If a secretary–typist with the aid of a word processor and other electronic equipment were to produce twice the output of office work she produced formerly, then obviously only half as many hours of work will be needed as before to produce the total output of office work. Unless the work week is cut by half, employment of secretary–typists will be cut in half.[2]

The second source of concern arises from the *notion that microelectronic technology is something more than another phase in the evolution of technology*. It is recognised that very significant technological changes have taken place since the Industrial Revolution, and although they eliminated some jobs, on the whole they were accompanied or were followed by rapid job creation. Microelectronics is deemed to be different: it is pervasive in application – there is hardly any work activity to which some form of microelectronic process would not be appropriate – and it has a comparatively large productive capacity. 'No technology in history', writes Colin Norman, 'has had such a broad range of potential applications in the workplace'.[3]

The third source of concern are reports from individual industries and processes which indicate *increases in productivity of 10 to 15 times* the rates obtained with electromechanical technology. It is difficult to imagine how such very significant increase in productivity can be offset by increases in demand or decreases in hours of work.

The fourth source of concern is the notion that unlike electromechanical technology, which has a complementary functional relationship to labour, *microelectronic technology is conceived independent of labour participation in many of the activities it performs* – computers, computer-related instruments and telecommunications technologies are conceived linked together into integrated networks performing wide-ranging functions without human intervention.

Are the Concerns Justified?

The historical record suggests they are not. Over time goods and services have changed very substantially in amounts, qualities and mix. Their production involved changes in technology and processes, which dictated changes in occupations, labour–capital ratios, and labour–output ratios. The labour intensity of production decreased in varying degrees amongst the multitude of production processes in the economy at large, and output per unit of time increased in varying degrees. But, employment on the aggregate increased almost continuously. Whether this increase in employment *was functionally related* to the output of goods and services or whether some of it *was facilitated* by the increase in the output of goods and services is an issue worthy of careful consideration.

Regarding the nature of microelectronic technology, I take the view that in the context of the currently prevailing social and economic technostructure it is no different in its implications for society, the economy and employment than were all major technologies in the context of the social and economic environments within which they were introduced. The now primitive technologies of the late 1700s and early 1800s probably had a more dramatic impact on the then existing social and economic technostructure than can be expected of microelectronic technology in our situation. The levels of education of the population at large are different, and most significantly, the population at large has a technical orientation in its daily work and leisure activities. Even though microelectronic technology departs significantly in some respects from the electromechanical technology to which the people are accustomed, there is no evidence to date of any implications for society, the economy and employment that differ notably from the implications of electromechanical technology. Changes are taking place; some very significant. But, changes have taken place in the past, some of them very significant, too. The computer-related changes have not been notably different in their impacts from major electromechanical changes of the historical past.

Evidence of Negative Employment Effects

To-date, there has been no serious effort to determine the possible effect of microelectronic technology on employment generally – on the aggregate. A few widely quoted British studies[4] make general references to future negative effects, and some of them purport to estimate the total employment effect for Britain, under various assumptions, but the statistical information on which the estimates are based and the statistical analysis to which the information is subjected are such as to cause justifiable doubt about their validity.

The studies reporting negative employment effects have been industry case studies: the Siemens Company study on the potential impact on office jobs; the Nora and Minc study on employment in banking and insurance; the National Cash Register Company report on employment in the firm; employment in the Swiss watch industry; and many other.

Since these and some other industry studies are often presented as examples of what should be expected in industries and processes in the economy at large, a brief reference to each may be warranted:

1 The Swiss Watch Industry: employment decreased by 46 000 during the 1970s.[5] Although the implication is that the advent of microelectronic technology has been responsible for it, in reality responsibility rests with the failure of the industry to apply the new technology, and the resultant loss of markets to the Japanese and US industries.
2 Telex Machines: microprocessors increased the capacity of telex machines and reduced significantly the labour required in their production and maintenance. The model produced by Standard Electric Lorenz of West Germany required 18 hours for its manufacture compared to 75 hours for its mechanical or electromechanical counterpart. One microprocessor replaced 936 moving technical parts.[6]
3 Electronic Cash Registers: the National Cash Register Co. (US) reported in its 1975 Annual Report that its electronic cash registers required only one-quarter as much labour to produce as did their mechanical or electromechanical counterparts. As a result, employment was reduced from 37 000 in 1970 to 18 000 in 1975.[7]
4 Telecommunications Equipment: the Swedish firm Telecommunications Ericsson reduced its work force from 15 000 in 1975 to 10 000 in 1978; and employment in the manufacture of telecommunications equipment in Britain fell from 88 000 in 1975 to 65 000 in 1978.[8]
5 The Printing Industry: computerised typesetting, word processors and other electronic instruments and processes have had serious negative employment effects on printing trades. In West Germany, employment decreased 21.3 per cent between 1970 and 1977, while productivity increased 43.5 per cent.[9] It is expected that office automation and electronic mail will have further negative employment effects in the industry.[10]
6 Office Employment: the Siemens study 'Office 1990' allegedly examined 2.7 million office jobs to determine the extent to which they can be standardised and automated. In public administration 75

percent of all jobs could be standardised and 38 per cent automated; while in the private sector 25–38 per cent of all jobs could be automated.[11] The evident decision of the Siemens Corporation not to release the report casts considerable doubt on the validity of the reported findings. There is other evidence, of course, of significant increases in office efficiency as a result of the application of microelectronic technology. A report from the Earth Resources Research Institute of London indicated that the substitution of typewriters with word processors increased efficiency by as much as 400 per cent 'where the flow of work had been continuous.'[12] Furthermore, it is generally expected that efficiency will increase further when office technology becomes integrated into electronic systems which will store, transport and process information continuously, 24 hours per day.

7 Banking and Insurance: The Nora/Minc report[13] is often quoted for its statement that employment in banking and insurance will decrease by up to 30 per cent by 1988. But, seldom is reference made to the authors' qualification that competition from other domestic financial institutions and from foreign sources will contribute to the decline in employment.

8 The Automobile Industry: the work of welding and painting robots is well known to all. It is expected that by 1990 a large number of assembly work-functions will be performed by robots. In addition, design and testing functions will be performed increasingly by computers. A 1978 study by the Society of Manufacturing Engineers and the University of Michigan[14] concluded that:

(a) by 1998, 'programmable automation will replace half the direct labour in assembly of small components';

(b) by 1990, industrial robots will perform 'many of the job tasks now handled by assembly workers';

(c) by 1990, '50 per cent of the workforce on the floor will be highly skilled and trained engineers and technicians keeping automated, robotised and computerised plants operating';

(d) by 1995, '50 per cent of the direct labour in automobile final assembly will be replaced by programmable automation'.

9 Manufacture of Calculators: a report on employment at the Olivetti Company[15] indicates that the production of a mechanical calculator (Divisumma 24 model) involved *nine* working hours of labour; the production of an electronic calculator (Logos 50) with performance similar to that of the mechanical calculator involved *five* hours of labour; and the production of an electronic printing calculator with

microcircuits requires *half-an-hour* of labour. Evidently, the labour intensity of production decreased 95 per cent. Similarly, the production of a mechanical accounting machine (Olivetti Audit 24) took 33 hours of labour; the corresponding electronic model took 13 hours of labour; and it is expected that the introduction of microprocessors will reduce the labour requirement significantly.

What do these industry case studies tell us? *They tell us that microelectronic technology tends to reduce significantly the labour intensity of production of certain goods and services heretofore produced by electromechanical technology, and that the labour input required for the production of certain microelectronic products is significantly less than the labour input required for the production of their electromechanical counterparts.* As a result, it is alleged that significant numbers of workers have been or are expected to be displaced from their jobs.

But, there is much that most of the studies do not tell us. They do not tell us what happened to the employment of non-production workers – administrative, managerial, professional and technical. The employment of such workers increased significantly in the past 20 years in every advanced industrial country, which period happens to coincide with a significant increase in the employment of microelectronic technology. Also, the studies do not tell us about the nature and volume of output after the introduction of microelectronic technology – the new products and services facilitated by the new technology – and the relationship of total employment to it. In an investigation of the employment effects of word processors, we found that the increase in productivity was more than offset by additional work, and by work activities which could not have been undertaken by the conventional manual and electromechanical processes.[16] Evidence that the application of microelectronic technology in the production of a given product or service increased productivity by 300, 400 or 1000 per cent does not in itself mean that employment will fall. It is conceivable that demand for the product and total output will increase by the same proportion as the increase in productivity, in which case employment *at the production level* will remain unchanged. In addition, an increase in output of that magnitude will likely have positive employment effects on non-production workers responsible for its management, and positive employment effects in processes throughout the economy which are linked to the output through the supply of materials and the provision of transportation, storage, sales, finance, repair and other services. Consider, for example, an increase in the output of automobiles by 100 or 200 per cent with the existing labour force. It will mean an increase of equal magnitude in all produced materials entering into the production of automobiles – steel, aluminium, tires, glass, etc. Furthermore, an increase in demand of that magnitude will cause an increase in demand for services – financial, insurance, repair and maintenance, etc. As indicated above, all of these must be taken into account to determine the net employment effect on the aggregate.

An aspect of microelectronic technology with positive employment implications which escapes attention in productivity measurements is the production of *new goods and services*. Productivity measures input–output changes of specific goods and services produced over specified periods of time. It does not take into account the introduction of new products. Yet, new products have important employment implications. For example, the information on the Olivetti case would lead one to conclude that employment declined. It is unlikely that sales of electronic printing calculators would increase the required twenty times to offset the 95 per cent reduction in the labour input per unit of output. But, the report also states that microelectronic technology has facilitated an extraordinary increase in the range of products: in 1965 the company produced 95 products; in 1977–78 it produced 600 products. Rapid changes in the technology apparently dictate frequent changes in processes and products, which in turn dictate a greater product mix for stability in market sales. In addition, in a period of rapid innovation, continuous product modifications are necessary to remain competitive. The average commercial product life of Olivetti mechanical calculators was 15 years; the average product life of the electronic machines is 2–3 years. Such short life requires continuous research and development work.

Changes in productivity and employment of the nature detailed in the industry case studies are not unique to microelectronic technology. The indicated rates of change may appear somewhat greater, and the time periods over which they have been achieved may appear somewhat shorter, than changes associated with mechanical and electromechanical technology, but an examination of the recent historical record casts some doubt on such impressions. For example,

1 *Employment in US agriculture* fell by close to two million workers between 1947 and 1957; by a further 2.1 million between 1957 and 1967; and by another 600,000 between 1967 and 1971. While employment was falling sharply, the volume of output was rising at the rate of about 50 per cent per decade, resulting in productivity increases of almost 100 per cent per decade.

2 *The replacement of copper and galvanised pipes with plastic pipes*, and changes in methods of pipe connections increased productivity in certain pipe installations as much as sevenfold. Before the introduction of the new materials and processes it took a journeyman plumber and an apprentice seven days of work time to complete an average house; it now takes approximately one day.

3 *The electromechanisation of certain household activities*, and changes in the social status of occupations brought about the demise of the domestic servant as an occupation. As late as the 1920s domestic servants, coachmen, butlers, lodging and boarding housekeepers, charworkers and cleaners, cooks, housekeepers, matrons and stewards constituted very substantial proportions of total employment. In Britain, about 1.4 million women and 45 000 men were employed as 'indoor domestic servants' in 1911.[17] By contrast, the occupation of typist and stenographer was virtually unknown. If anyone had said at that time that employment in domestic service will decline significantly over time, and virtually disappear as an occupation within a lifetime, it would have created considerable concern about employment opportunities for an important segment of the then existing female labour force. Yet, over a period equivalent to that which we now attempt to cover in our forecasts, predictions and visions, the employment of domestic servants virtually disappeared, the employment of typists and stenographers increased fifty times and more, and the advent of recording devices brought about the demise of the stenographic work function.

4 *The evolution of typing technology*, from mechanical to electromechanical, improvements in methods of correcting typed work, and the introduction of duplicating machines increased productivity in typing by more than 100 per cent. Yet, employment of typists more than doubled over the past two decades.

These examples illustrate two important realities: one is that employment *in individual processes* is not determined by the rate of increase in productivity taken by itself; it is determined by the rate of increase in productivity relative to the rate of increase in the volume of output. If productivity were to increase 100 per cent, and demand, and hence the volume of output were to also increase 100 per cent employment will remain unchanged. Employment will decrease when productivity increases faster than demand and the rate of increase in the volume of output, and it will increase when the volume of output increases faster than the rate of increase in productivity. In relation to typing, the information suggests that the volume of typing services increased considerably faster than the 100 per cent increase in productivity, resulting in a substantial increase in employment, whereas the information in relation to agriculture suggests that the volume of output increased substantially less than the rate of increase in productivity, resulting in the considerable decrease in employment. An examination of productivity and employment in manufacturing over the past two decades will establish that productivity has been rising somewhat faster than the rate of increase in the volume of output, resulting in a progressively lower and lower rate of increase in employment. This sort of evidence from most advanced industrial nations caused Christopher Freeman to suggest the possible onset of 'jobless growth.'[18] It is not inconceivable for microelectronic technology, in the form of computer-aided design (CAD)/computer-aided manufacturing (CAM) systems to increase productivity so substantially more than the increase in demand and the volume of manufacturing output, as to cause rapid and significant decreases of employment in manufacturing. But, such a development need not necessarily usher the onset of jobless growth in the economy as a whole, even though it may do so in manufacturing. Account must be taken of the employment effects of growth on the aggregate.

The second reality is that technology creates new products, new processes, new services and thereby generates new employments and new occupations. The advent of the internal combustion engine brought the demise of employments related to horses and carriages, but created employments in the production, repair and maintenance, and operation of motor vehicles. Grooms became chauffeurs; carters and coachmen became bus drivers; blacksmiths became mechanics. As to domestic servants, they found greater freedom and more regular hours in the rapidly expanding demand for office workers.

The Possibility of 'Jobless Growth'

The possibility that microelectronic technology is ushering a period of jobless growth is an issue of cardinal importance. To a nation experiencing an increasing labour force, it could mean massive involuntary unemployment.

The jobless growth thesis is based on three developments: (1) the very significant decrease in the labour intensity of production processes in agriculture, and the resultant decrease of employment in the industry; (2) the increasing evidence that employment in manufacturing and other goods-producing industries has reached a plateau in most advanced industrial countries, and the certain expectation that the introduction of microelectronic processes will reduce it in absolute terms; and (3) the anticipated decrease in the labour intensity of services-producing processes, consequent on the introduction of microelectronic instruments and telematic systems.

These are valid premises, based on evidence: in the United States, employment in agriculture appears to have stabilised at around 3.4 million; in mining it has ranged between 600,000 and one million since 1950; and in manufacturing it has stood at around 20 million in most of the past 15 years. The total numbers employed in these goods-producing processes have been remarkably stable for a goods-producing economy such as the American: in 1950, the total was 23.3 million; in 1960, it was 23.0 million; in 1970, 23.5 million, and in 1980, 24.7 million. It is problematical whether we can realistically expect any significant increase of employment in goods-production; which means that the proportion of the labour force to be employed in goods-production can be expected to continue its historical decline.[19] It is quite possible that by the end of this century only about 10–15 per cent of the US labour force will be engaged in the production of goods. Tom Stonier has made a similar statement in relation to Great Britian: 'It is highly probable', he said, 'that by early in the next century it will require no more than 10 per cent of the labour force to provide us with all material goods.'[20] But, should this concern us? Considering that the decrease in the proportion of the labour force engaged in the production of material goods has been a historical reality, further decreases should not, in themselves, be a source of concern. The concern should focus on growth in goods-production; not whether the growth has been achieved with less and less labour. Growth will provide employment elsewhere, in the services-producing sector of the economy, as it has done over the past 30–40 years.

An important question, which is the source of most concerns about the overall employment effect of microelectronic technology, is what is likely to happen to employment in the service sector – the sector that absorbed most of the increase in the labour force in the past 30 years. Is it possible that services-producing processes will gradually become as capital intensive as goods-producing processes have become? The possibility of jobless growth in services is the critical issue. Should this happen, demand for human labour can be expected to decline significantly over time.

What is the possibility of employment in services-producing activities declining or stabilising at current levels?[21] There is a strong possibility that employment in *existing* services-producing activities will decline. The introduction of microelectronic instruments and processes will reduce the labour intensity of most processes, in the same way as mechanical and electromechanical instruments and processes reduced the labour intensity in agriculture, mining and manufacturing. In some activities, demand and the output of services will increase sufficiently to offset or more than offset the increase in productivity, and thereby sustain employment at existing levels or even increase it. But, it should be expected that many of the major service activities, which provided employment to increasing proportions of the labour force over the past 30 years, such as office activities and sales activities, will record decreasing employment capacities. On the other hand, there are many socially desirable services, in education, health, recreation, political activity, that have not been provided at all or have been provided in inadequate supply relative to the needs of society at large; and the quality of many services has been lower, in some instances considerably lower, than professionally established norms. The elimination of such gaps and deficiencies can create very substantial employment. The major limiting factor heretofore has been the capacity of economies to generate the required resources.

Functional Relationships Between Growth and Jobs

What is the functional relationship between growth and jobs? Is job-creation a condition for growth, or is it facilitated by growth? In other words, is all employment necessary for the growth process itself, or is some of it the result of growth, in the sense that growth facilitates the creation of paid employment as an end in itself? As a social and political objective? When the government decides to establish a China desk in the foreign office and assigns to it a group of political, social and military specialists, is that necessary for the process of economic growth or is it simply facilitated by income creating growth?

Given the possibility that growth both *creates* jobs that are functionally related to the production processes, and *facilitates* the creation of jobs not so related, then the *issue of concern should be growth itself* and not whether the growth is or is not accompanied by the creation of jobs functionally related to it.[22] In such case, to the extent that microelectronic technology will increase productivity and growth, it will both *create* and *facilitate* the creation of jobs.

The problem is growth; not any lack of socially desirable work activities. There are scores of potential work activities, particularly in the social field, which are not being performed not because they will not contribute to net economic and social welfare, but because of limited resources. Assuming microelectronic technology increases the resources available to the economy and society at large, there would be no problem in creating socially desirable employment.

The Record of Aggregate Employment

The joblessness that most advanced industrial countries experience currently, is related to negative output and negative productivity on the aggregate, not to positive productivity implied in the jobless growth thesis. An examination of the United States record since 1965, which is a period of increasing utilisation of microelectronic technology, will establish very significant increases in employment: in the period 1965–1970 total employment increased from 71.1 million to 78.7 million or by 7.6 million; between 1970 and 1975 it increased by another 7.1 million to 85.8 million in 1975; between 1975 and 1980 it increased by a further13.5 million, to 99.3 million in 1980. At the end of 1981, total employment stood at 100.4 million, an increase of almost 30 million within the relatively short period of 16 years. On the face of this reality, in a period of rapid implementation of automated and semi-automated mechanical, electromechanical, electronic, microelectronic and communication instruments and processes, it must be agonisingly difficult to propagate skepticism about the capacity of an advanced industrial–commercial economy to create employment on the aggregate. Agony is reduced significantly, of course, when skepticism is founded on ignorance.

Where did those 30 million men and women find employment? 9.6 million found employment in non-government services-producing enterprises and institutions; 6.0 million were taken into employment by federal, state and local governments; close to 8 million found employment in wholesale and retail trade; finance, insurance and real estate enterprises took close to 2.3 million; manufacturing provided employment to 2.1 million; and transportation and public utilities employed 1.1 million.

How can we account for this very substantial growth in employment during a period of increasing and widespread application of microelectronic technology? We know that thousands of work functions have been eliminated by computers and computer-related instruments and processes – functions related to accounting processes, payroll administration, the maintenance of personnel records, inventory administration, and generally functions related to the storage, manipulation and retrieval of information; and we know also that banks and other financial institutions, insurance and real estate companies, major transportation companies, and most large enterprises and institutions have established varying forms of computer and telecommunications networks, which have had negative employment effects on certain employments. Yet, the overall effect on employment has been positive. The explanation for this will be found in two major adjustments: one is the functional relationships, substitutions and additions of new goods and services; and the other will be found in changes in the hours actually worked by people with jobs.

Reference was made earlier to Joseph Schumpeter's characterisation of technological change as the process of creative destruction. It destroys processes, products and services, and it creates processes, products and services; the organisations and structures of commercial, industrial and institutional enterprises change, the range and nature of work functions change, and the nature and structure of occupations and employments change. For example, the organisation and structure of agriculture in 1981 is vastly different from the predominantly family farm organisation of the 1920s or even 1950s: employment in agriculture has fallen significantly over time, but the decrease has been perhaps more than offset by increases of employment in enterprises, institutions and activities *functionally related* to agriculture, such as, manufacturing of farm machinery and equipment; distributing machinery, equipment and supplies; manufacturing fertilisers and chemical products used in agriculture; agricultural research activities, and farm consultative services of all kinds; and governmental and institutional departments and agencies. Upon the examination of these functional relationships, and associated supplementary, supportive and ancillary production activities, it will be determined that in reality employment in agriculture did not decrease; the industrial and occupational structure of employment changed. Millions of farm workers who worked with hand-operated implements and used animals in work activities, became industrial, commercial and service workers, in activities related to agriculture.

In 1945, the International Business Machines Company of the United States employed 17 500 people, the 3M Company employed 6795 and the Xerox Corporation employed 593. In 1974, IBM employed 292 350, 3M employed 83 609, and Xerox employed 101 380. The equipment produced by these enterprises contributed to changes in production processes, in work-functions and employments, brought about improvements in productivity, generated new manufacturing, distributive, consultative and service enterprises, created additional employment and caused employment in some enterprises to decline. But, on the whole, when account is taken of all functional relationships throughout the economy and society, commercial and non-commercial, it will be found that more jobs have been created than destroyed. 'More jobs' does not necessarily mean, of course, more work. That is an issue to which we direct our attention now.

The Hours of Work Adjustment

The average U.S. worker worked substantially fewer hours in 1981 than in 1951: hours of work per day and per week have decreased by only about 10 per cent; but the number of statutory holidays has increased; annual holiday periods have increased; and maternity leaves, education and training leaves, sick leave allowances, and discretionary times off have become longer and more frequent. In addition, the proportion of the labour force engaged in part-time employment has almost doubled to about 14 per cent in 1981. As much as 40 per cent of the increase in employment since 1951 can be accounted by the decrease in hours worked by workers on the average annually.

It is not the hours of work worked per week that matter; it is rather the hours of work worked over the year or over the years. The hours of work worked per day, per week or per month may remain the same, but the total hours worked over the year will vary because of changes in annual holidays, statutory holidays, sick leave, discretionary time off, educational leaves, maternity leaves, and other times off work for various reasons. It is the times off work that reduce the volume of time worked, not the reduction in hours per day or week. The hours per week have remained relatively stable over the past two decades, in the range of 37–40; but the hours actually worked on the average have fallen about 20 per cent. This is the adjustment to technology and rising living standards. People will continue to work the regular hours, but will take time off work more frequently to engage in activities they like, such as travel, study, attend conferences, and engage in recreational and cultural activities.

The reality underscores the positive employment effects of technological change, economic growth, and rising productivity. The concurrent experience of less work and a higher standard of living means that workers took their share of the increase in productivity partly in the form of higher wages and salaries, and partly in the form of a decrease in hours of work. A decrease in hours of work when the labour intensity of production processes is decreasing (productivity is rising) is, of course, a form of work sharing. The difference between this kind of work sharing and the work sharing advocated in periods of economic stagnation and excessive unemployment is that this is sharing in growth, whereas the work sharing in periods of excessive unemployment is sharing in misery. Therefore, the decrease in labour intensity of work, which is commonly attributed to technology, is in fact facilitated by the increase in efficiency of production.

The issue of decreasing hours gives rise, of course, to the question of some limit to their decrease. Since the number of hours is finite, it means at the extreme zero hours. This is not an inconceivable outcome ultimately, but in the meantime we can expect gradual reductions in the average hours worked over the year, as vacation periods increase, educational leaves become common, maternity (and paternity) leaves become a regular phenomenon, and discretionary time off increases. All of these are a common practice presently in some employments, and given an increase in the capacity of the economy to pay, there would be no reason, indeed it would be difficult to resist the pressure for their extension to other employments. It was reported recently that at the 1982 conference of government leaders at Versailles, President Mitterand of France indicated that consideration was being given to a system of sabbaticals for all workers after 10 years of work. Such an arrangement would mean that every year one-tenth of a nation's labour force would be off work. Adding to that time-off the time off work by the rest of the labour force, for annual holidays, maternity leaves, education leaves, sick leaves, and statutory holidays, the average annual hours per worker will fall very significantly. This is not an unlikely development. It is predicated on increasing productivity and economic growth. If we were to assume that microelectronic technology will indeed bring about growth, the historical experience suggests an outcome of decreasing hours of work and increasing employment.

If the other two factors of production, land and capital, can produce increasing quantities of goods and services with only limited participation from the human factor, there would be no reason that the human factor should participate as actively as it participates currently. It is significant to note that we each have at our disposal 5824 hours of waking time per year. Since we allocate to actual work only about 1800 hours per year on the average, we have 4024 hours for allocation to other activities and leisure. The fact that working people generally seek further reductions in work time indicates an expectation on the average of greater pleasure from the increment in discretionary time, than from the foregone increment in income. Given a restoration of productivity and growth to satisfactory levels, and given sustained performance at such levels over a number of years, the hours worked can be expected to decrease sufficiently to accommodate the projected increases in the labour force. To repeat, it is growth that should be our concern, not the possibility of it being jobless.

The Process of Change

The historical evolution of processes, industrial and institutional structures, inter-industry functional relationships, occupations, employments and hours worked, suggest that change is a natural and continuing phenomenon. There is no conceivable reason to expect the survival of currently existing industries, production processes, occupations, employments and work functions. There is no conceivable reason that banking, for example, should remain an important source of employment, and that secretarial work functions should remain unchanged, or indeed, that the occupation of secretary should not disappear. Most of the occupations and employments which today constitute significant proportions of the labour force have evolved within the past 40 years. It is quite conceivable that over the next 40 years new occupations and employments will predominate. Is there any reason not to allow this to happen? Is there any reason to want to protect existing employments? What is so exciting about having hundreds of thousands of women engaged in the daily drudgery of office work? What is so exciting about standing at a cash register and monotonously, hour upon hour, registering numerical values?

It is not change that we should be concerned about; it is the rate of change. We have not had any adverse employment effects from microelectronic technology to date, because the rate of implementation has been relatively slow. The changes, even though very significant, have been almost imperceptible. Some employment activities have disappeared, new processes have been established; computer technology has become almost commonplace. Yet, there is no evidence of disruptive change that one commonly associates with a revolutionary change.

Concluding Comment

We wrote above that the reality of economic processes on the aggregate is much different from the 'logic' underlying extrapolations from single developments, even when those developments, like the advent of microelectronic technology, have pervasive characteristics. Care must be exercised to not generalise on the basis of limited premises.

Whether computers, computer-related instruments and telecommunications technology are ushering a leisure society remains an issue of uncertainty at this time. There is increasing evidence of very significant reductions in the labour intensity of production in both goods-producing and services-producing processes. Goods and services are being produced with labour inputs as low as 20 per cent of the quantities used prior to the introduction of electronic processes, and electronic instruments are being produced with as little as 5 per cent of the labour inputs it took to produce their electromechanical counterparts. The production capacity of the technology is so vast, its potential efficiency so great, and its pervasiveness so comprehensive as to make it virtually impossible to offset through increases in aggregate demand even over the longer run. New goods and services will be produced, as in the past; some existing goods and services will be produced in much larger quantities; some new occupations and employments will emerge, as in the past; some of the work-functions of existing occupations and employments will change; and some existing occupations and employments will increase in number. But, it is highly problematical that these developments will offset the expected decrease of labour intensity in most production processes in the economy at large. Other things being equal, this would mean increasing involuntary unemployment. But, we have noted an important adjusting variable in the actual participation of people in work activity. Participation rates, defined in terms of people participating actively in economic activity, are less significant to the productivity–employment relationship than the number of hours the participants allocate to actual work activity over a period of a year, five years or over a lifetime of work. The period of lifetime of work has been shortening because of increasing delays in entry and increasingly early exits from the labour market, and will likely shorten more as incomes increase, and the continuity of work over a lifetime will likely be interrupted more frequently than heretofore by educational leaves, sabbaticals, and discretionary time off. A recent U.S. study on retirement amongst professional, managerial and technical workers found that amongst those who retired in 1968–69 only 13 per cent retired before age 60. Amongst those retired in 1976–77, 30 per cent retired before age 60.[23]

The record indicates that the decrease in hours actually worked by people has been a very significant variable in the productivity-employment relationship. Evidently, substantial increases in productivity have been distributed in the form of decreases in hours of work, paid holidays and vacations. This will remain a major adjusting variable to the productivity increases expected from microelectronic technology. In view of the finite nature of time per day, week, year or years of potential work life, this does suggest the ultimate possibility of zero hours in *economic* activities for the majority of the population. But, such an eventuality will not necessarily be regarded negatively: if the other factors of production can produce the outputs of goods and services necessary for a rising standard of living of the population at large, there would be no conceivable reason for the participation of the human factor in the economic process. The problems that would arise from this will be social and political—the psycho-social need for work, and the distribution of the national output amongst people at large. Employment as we now have it is a convenient way of distributing the national output, even though of questionable merit from the standpoint of equity. As to the psycho-social need for work, the very significant decrease in the hours actually worked, and the quest for more time off work suggest that people have become accustomed to working less and less.

Increases in productivity and total output increase the ability to pay and thereby facilitate increases in real incomes, decreases in hours of work, and decreases in work-loads. We know that real incomes have generally risen over the past 40 years; hours of work have fallen considerably; and work-loads have decreased. The effect of these on employment was to increase it very substantially. As long as production and total output continue to increase, and adjustments to hours worked and work-loads continue to be effected, there is no reason not to expect a continuing capacity to provide full employment. The failures to sustain satisfactory levels of employment in recent years, in most advanced industrial nations, reflect failure to sustain satisfactory levels of productivity and growth. Should the application of microelectronic instruments and processes restore satisfactory levels of productivity and growth, employment will be restored to satisfactory levels, too.

9 Work and Leisure

The Concept of Work

What is 'work?'[1] The question is fundamental at a time when it is increasingly asserted that the integration of computers and telecommunications technology in production processes will make work increasingly more scarce. But, what work? The work to which reference is made in this context is usually limited to activities associated with the production of goods and services for which payments are made. But, there is a problem with this: there are many work activities which produce goods and services, such as those related to home and family, and voluntary services rendered to churches, clubs, public service organisations, health and welfare institutions, and there are equally many activities which are classified as work under certain conditions and not work under other conditions. For example, the activities of professional athletes and artists are deemed to be work, while the activities of amateur athletes and artists are not so deemed, even though the time allocated to the activities and the intensity and effort involved in them may be the same. What is the difference? Essentially it is that one group performs its activities for money while the other does not.[2] The moment that the amateur begins to perform for money the activities become work. This suggests that it is not the nature of activity that determines whether it is or it is not work, but rather whether a direct payment is made for the performance of the activity.

The possibility that microelectronic technology will facilitate the production of increasing quantities of goods and services with decreasing quantities of labour raises the question of alternative forms of employment and alternative work activities. One of the major difficulties encountered in efforts to determine the possible alternative forms of employment and alternative work activities is *the concept of work*. What are the distinctive characteristics of employment work and work not recognised as employment? Is it possible that work not recognised as employment at present will be so recognised in future years? We know that microelectronic technology, like other technologies in the historical past, will generate new processes, products and services, which will involve new work activities; and we also know that changes in means of communication will impact on relations amongst people and between people and commercial, industrial and institutional enterprises. What work activities will emerge from these changed relationships?

The Economist's Concept of Work

The economist's concept of work is limited to those activities only which are performed for an actual or implicit payment. People are deemed to work, in an economic sense, if they are working for pay or profit, or their work is associated with a farm or business enterprise operated by a related member of the family. Implicit in this definition is the assumption of a contribution to output. Economic logic dictates that an activity cannot be work if it does not contribute to the output. When payment is made for an activity, it is implicitly assumed that the payment reflects the contribution of the recipient to the value of the output. If the recipient has made no contribution, then the payment will be at the expense of someone who has made a contribution, or at the expense of one of the other factors of production.

This presents a *problem* and a *possibility*. The *problem* is with the identification and measurement of contributions to output. With goods, and the labour employed directly in their production, there is no particular difficulty; and the same can be said to some extent about all marketable services. But in many instances it is very difficult to relate individual activities to the output, and measurement of the contributions is doubly difficult. For example, what is the contribution to the national output of a civil servant monitoring developments in Poland and El Salvador; or of an advertising executive experimenting with a new toothpaste advertisement which will increase sales by 10 per cent at the expense of another toothpaste; or of a public relations person whose work functions are to develop and maintain a favourable public image for the enterprise, regardless of the nature of activities in which the enterprise is engaged? To the extent that they do not make any contributions to the output, their employment and payments to them will come from the contributions of other workers and the contributions of the other factors.

There is then the problem of deciding which contributions enter the output and which do not enter. When payment for an activity is the criterion determining work and by implication contribution, then the act of payment itself becomes the determinant of the contribution, not the activity that is being performed. Thus, the valueless activity, in an economic sense, of an amateur acquires value upon the payment of a salary; and the valueless activity of a hospital volunteer acquires value upon the payment of a wage, and the consequent change in classification from volunteer to employee. The activity remains unchanged; yet the output associated with the activity is regarded a contribution to a total output under one classification and not under another. As long as a political functionary renders services to the party organisation on a voluntary basis he/she is deemed not to contribute to the national output; but the moment the party gets hold of some funds and begins to pay for the services, the services become work, and the payment is deemed to reflect a contribution to the national output.

The problem is then to determine which activities make contributions, and which do not. The *possibility* is, that many of the activities for which payments are made, and as a consequence are deemed to be work activities, do not in fact make any contribution to output. The creation of such activities is determined by ability to pay, they do not determine ability to pay; and payments for such activities are made from the contributions to output of other work activities, and the contributions of the other factors of production.

The role of technology in production processes is to increase factor productivities and thereby cause an outward movement of the production frontier. This suggests the possibility that the national output can be increased with decreasing participation by labour inputs. A critical question is how much of each factor of production – land, labour and capital – is necessary for the production of increasing quantities of the national output. The historical record indicates that increasing quantities of output have been produced with decreasing quantities of the labour factor. It is within the realm of possibility that the output of goods and services necessary for human existence and a rising standard of living will be produced with only minimal participation by the labour factor.

The critical issue in relation to the participation of labour in the production of the national output is the proportion of the national output that is necessary to sustain an increasing productive capacity in the economy. In other words, how much of the national output can be taken away from the factors that participate in its production without impairing their productive capacities. That amount will determine the payments that can be made to those who do not participate, and those whose work activities are motivated by social, cultural and political concerns rather than economic. This proposition gives implicit recognition to what I believe to be a reality, namely, that although all employment is related to output in a *distributive sense*, which means employment gives the right to a share of the output, all of it is not so related in a *functionally-productive sense*. Considerable employment owes its existence and is related to the capacities of industrial, commercial and institutional enterprises to pay. When the capacity to pay diminishes, as it happens in periods of inadequate growth, the creation of such employment ceases. When growth resumes, so does the growth of such employments.

The proposition is not fundamentally different from the Marxian and Physiocratic views on the production of surplus value.[3] But it differs significantly with respect to the sources of surplus value and the distribution of it. Marx attributed the surplus value to labour alone, and had it taken away by the capitalist; whereas the Physiocrats attributed it to the land and those involved in agricultural work activities, and had it taken away by the landlord. The proposition here is that the surplus output is the result of the application of all factors of production functionally associated with the production processes. The allocation of the surplus is for the most part directed towards the attainment of social and political objectives, one of which is the creation of employment.

The association of all employment with production of marketable goods and services has had a limiting influence on efforts to create employment. The work activities to be created had to be justified on the basis of their contribution to output, and payment for the performance of the activities had to be justified on the basis of the expected contributions by whoever performed the work activities. Such determinants of work, pay, and employment left many potential social service activities not undertaken, and many people not employed – not because the activities could not be justified on grounds of economic and social welfare, but because they could not be justified on the basis of standard economic value-added criteria, or because the minimum payments required by law, custom or contract could not be justified on the basis of expected contributions to the value of output. Hence, questions have arisen whether it is justified from the standpoint of net economic welfare to limit work activities to those only that are functionally related to processes producing goods and services. Should we not, as Margaret Mead put it, 'devise a system in which every individual's participation in society is such that he has dignity and purpose, and the society has a rationale for distributing the results of its high productivity'.[4] Whether we should, indeed, whether it would be possible to design, implement and sustain such a system will depend on whether the 'high productivity' can be attained again and sustained over time. To the extent that microelectronic technology will make that possible, it would then be possible to create a system of participation in social and economic activity based on both functionally productive and distributive criteria.

Changes in the Allocation of Time

Each of us has about sixteen hours of waking time per day, 112 hours per week. How is it used up? The average wage and salary earner allocates about 35 hours to paid *activities*, and the remainder to *unpaid activities* and *relaxation*. Technology effects the allocation of time to all activities, paid and unpaid, as well as amongst different forms of relaxation. Note, for example, the changes recorded between 1934 and 1966 in the allocation of time amongst certain activities and forms of relaxation.[5] (See Table 9.1.)

TABLE 9.1 *Allocation of time amongst unpaid activities, 1934 and 1966*

Unpaid Activities	*1934 (minutes per day)*	*1966 (minutes per day)*
Housework	95	140
Purposeful travel	129	76
Time spent shopping	16	34
Sub-total	240	250
Relaxation		
Meal-times	107	70
Visiting	26	46
Listening to radio	26	4
At the movies	22	3
Reading books	22	9
Walking for pleasure	22	1
Playing cards	9	4
Attending sports events	7	2
Correspondence	3	6
Watching television	0	90
Sub-total	244	235
Grand Total	484	485

SOURCE J. P. Robinson, *Social Change as measured by Time-Budgets*, mimeo paper, 1966 (Ref. 5).

It would appear technology influenced very significantly the allocation of *discretionary* time amongst activities and forms of relaxation: improvements in transportation almost halved the time allocated to purposeful travel, despite the substantial increase in urbanisation between 1934 and 1966, and the resultant increase in distances from work; changes in the physical structure of retailing establishments, and the considerable increase in varieties of goods available on the market, almost doubled the time allocated to shopping; and television caused havoc with the allocation of time to various forms of relaxation – meals, movies, radio, books, sports events, all lost time to television.

The time allocated to paid work activities now stands at only about 35 per cent of the total waking time available each week. Yet, people seek further reductions in it. This does not necessarily mean that people generally find the time allocated to paid work too much; it means rather that they want more discretionary time to themselves. It is quite conceivable that some or many of them will allocate some or all the additional discretionary time to more paid work of one kind or another. Flexibility in the allocation of time amongst activities and forms of relaxation appears to be the goal, not reduction in the time allocated to work activities. If this, indeed, is the goal, then microelectronic technology has very important implications. Indications are that patterns of work will change significantly, and human participation in work processes will become considerably more flexible than within mechanical processes.[6] It is widely expected, for example, that the introduction of a 'telematic' infrastructure will expand the range of activities performed from home considerably beyond what the telephone has facilitated. When the computer becomes the source of and intermediary for all information required for the performance of most work functions, and access to it becomes possible from any place, at any time, regular and routine visits to the place of the employer may no longer be necessary. This will save some of the time allocated to 'purposeful travel', which can be used in other work activities or relaxation.

The question 'what is work' has been answered implicitly: work is any activity which is not specifically classified as relaxation. Which means that the 112 hours of waking time available to each of us each week is allocated amongst four groups of activity: paid work activities, unpaid work activities (housework, church work, club work, volunteer work), leisure work activities (painting, gardening, and such other), and relaxation. Technology has effected the allocation of time amongst the four groups and within each group in the past, and indications are that it will do so in future. Indeed, Gershuny[7] suggests the possibility of some coalescence between certain household work activities and relaxation activities.

The concept of work has changed significantly over time; attitudes towards work have changed; the nature of work activities has changed; and work–output relationships have changed. Perhaps a new approach towards work and working is warranted, and the advent of microelectronic technology may compel the evolution of such a new approach.

The Concept of Leisure

There is a problem with the concept of 'leisure.' What is leisure? Aristotle distinguished between leisure and amusement. Leisure was the source of true happiness: 'And happiness is thought to depend on leisure; for we are busy that we may have leisure.'[8] Amusement was for refreshment so that exertion in work will be enhanced: 'Happiness, therefore, does not lie in amusement; it would indeed be strange if the end were amusement; . . . Relaxation, then, is not an end; for it is taken for the sake of activity.'[9] In other words, the need to unwind, to relieve tension.

We divide leisure time into *activity* and *relaxation*. The quest for more leisure time is for more discretionary activity time, not for more relaxation ('Consumption') time. The problem arises from the fact that traditionally time not allocated to productive activities, as defined by economists, has been deemed to be allocated to consumption. As Owen puts it: 'The definition of leisure time as consumption time emphasises the subjective intent with which an activity is approached, rather than the objective purpose which it serves.'[10] In Japan, the calesthenics in which workers engage daily are deemed part of the work activity; and in the Soviet Union, political indoctrination would be classified as participation in work activity. Most of us do our calesthenics and political learning at our leisure time. Are the activities production or consumption?

This question, whether leisure time which enhances economic welfare should be given a value and included in national income has been subject to considerable discussion. Simon Kuznets put the question this way:

> Considering that human life is short and that time spent on unpleasant tasks is a negative element, should we not insist that economic welfare and progress be measured not only in terms of

> supply of wanted goods but also in terms of freedom from unwanted labour?[11]

To the extent that work is a sacrifice, a disutility, an increase in leisure time will increase economic welfare. The additional pleasure gained from the additional leisure will more than offset the increment in output lost by the decrease in paid work time; and furthermore, to the extent that the leisure time is used up in amusement (in the sense used by Aristotle), productivity during work time will increase and offset some of the potential loss in output. Therefore, to the extent that leisure time contributes to an increase in economic welfare and output it should be given the value of work.

There is then the additional problem of distinguishing between work and leisure when the same activity is involved, and when the activity is performed with the same degree of intensity. Some people are deemed to work while training and playing hockey, football, golf, tennis, chess, cards, snooker, whereas others, similarly engaged are deemed to engage in leisure activity; and some people are deemed to work while engaged in activities related to painting, the playing of musical instruments, and performing on the stage, whereas others involved in the same activities are deemed not to work. What is the discriminating element? It is the assignment of a value to the activity, and the willingness of someone to pay that value. In a market economy, market forces assign values, and buyers determine who works and the amount of work. In non-market economies, governments, government agencies and social institutions assign values, make the requisite payments, and thereby determine who works. Therefore, the transformation of leisure activity into work activity appears to be a matter of assignment of value and payment for the activity. Many a casual 'leisure time' painter has been transformed into a working painter by a decision of government to fund a collection of paintings; the leisure activities of many musicians have been turned into work activities by government grants to orchestras; and philanthropic organisations have made it possible for many 'leisure' musical, writing, and acting activities to become work activities.

All this reveals a muddled reality about the concept of work. It is not the activity that is being defined, but rather the payment for the activity. Whether an activity is work or non-work, and whether an activity is work activity or leisure activity depends on whether someone is willing to pay for it. This means that *employment*, which by definition is limited to paid activities, is determined by the ability and willingness to pay for whatever activities people can perform.

The critical question here is the relationship between what people do and the ability to pay. If ability to pay is independent of the activities in which most of the people engage, that is, if economic growth and the resultant ability to pay is the result of non-human factors of production, then full employment can be maintained by the simple act of payment for activities which do not contribute to output, but which contribute to social welfare. Given social and political purpose to community existence, the activities could be stratified and payments made accordingly. This is not utopia, communist or any other. It is a reality that is being suggested as a possible outcome of the application of microelectronic technology to all production processes. The technology is expected to produce the surpluses which will facilitate the ability to pay for activities that are related to the general well-being of the population at large. Perhaps we are on the way to concepts of work and leisure that depart significantly from those in existence at present. Margaret Mead commented on the issue in the following way:

> One of our central problems at present is to begin to get rid of this dichotomy between work and leisure, between what you are paid to do, the way in which you get hold of a bit of the currency of a country, and your involvement in the country – between the right to experience the benefits, at a certain level of food, medical care, and education, and the possibility of using one's gifts to the limits.[12]

Attitudes Towards Work and Nature of Work

Attitudes towards work have varied widely through history. What work one did and did not do, and what work was appropriate and not appropriate, have been dictated by social norms founded on tradition, economic conditions, social structures, and religious doctrines. 'To the Greek mind' writes Alexander Gray 'nearly all activities of modern society would have appeared unworthy and debasing. When slaves are at hand to do the work, work becomes the mark of the slave.'[13] Similar attitudes have prevailed in socioeconomic systems governed by castes, and where large proportions of the population have existed at poverty levels. All physical work was deemed appropriate for the lower class, the slave, the domestic servant and the hired hand.

To Plato, Aristotle and Xenophon, husbandmen, builders, weavers, shoemakers, 'mechanics', and artificers of all kinds were indispensable to the existence of the State, but they could not be citizens. Citizenship was an art, requiring much study and many kinds of knowledge, which dictated that it be the primary occupation. To Cicero, most occupations were 'vulgar':

> Now in regard to trades and other means of livelihood, which ones are to be considered becoming to a gentleman and which ones are vulgar, we have been taught, in general, as follows: First, those means of livelihood are rejected as undesirable which incur people's ill-will, as those of tax-gatherers and usurers. Unbecoming to a gentleman, too, and vulgar, are the means of livelihood of all hired workmen whom we pay for mere manual labour, not for artistic skill; for in their case the very wages they receive is a pledge of their slavery. Vulgar we must consider those also who buy from wholesale merchants to retail immediately; for they would get no profits without a great deal of downright lying; and verily there is no action that is meaner than misrepresentation. And all mechanics are engaged in vulgar trades; for no workshop can have anything liberal about it. Least respectable of all are those trades which cater to sensual pleasures:
>
> Fishmongers, butchers, cooks, and poulterers, and fishermen, as Terrence says. Add to these, if you please, the perfumers, dancers, and the whole *corps de ballet*.
>
> But the professions in which either a higher degree of intelligence is required or from which no small benefit to society is derived – medicine and architecture, for example, and teaching – these are proper for those whose social position they become. Trade, if it is on a small scale, is to be considered vulgar; but if wholesale and on a large scale, importing large quantities from all parts of the world and distributing to many without misrepresentation, it is not to be greatly disparaged. Nay, it even seems to deserve the highest respect, if those who are engaged in it, satiated, or rather, I should say, satisfied with the fortunes they have made, make their way from the port to a country estate, as they have often made it from the sea into port. But of all the occupations by which gain is secured, none is better than agriculture, none more profitable, none more delightful, none more becoming to a freeman.[14]

This is, of course, a commentary on the social status of occupations and employments, not a commentary on the productivities and contributions to the national output of different occupations and employments. Nevertheless, the impression is conveyed that like the 'natural' and legal slaves in Aristotles' Greece,[15] the 'vulgar' occupations were regarded as nothing more than instruments of production. This raises two questions: one is whether there is any substantive difference between the attitude recorded by Cicero and the economist's concept of 'labour', and the other is whether it is possible that the national output can be produced without slaves and vulgar occupations, so that most of the people can be citizens and freemen. Equally, the slaves need not be human; they can be microelectronic.

Christianity postulated a doctrine totally opposed to the Greek and Roman views. God Himself worked, and rested from His work on the seventh day; Christ worked; and St. Paul worked day and night so that he may not be 'chargeable to anyone'.[16] Indeed, he laid down the rule, often attributed to Marx, that any man who would not work, neither should he eat. To work with ones own hands was dignified and noble; to labour was a duty.

Marx accepted fully the Christian dogma on the matter: to him work was 'the act of man's self creation, . . . not only a means to an end – the product – but an end in itself, the meaningful expression of human energy. . . . only in being productively active can man make sense of his life'.[17] He believed that work should be the most important source of human enjoyment, but to make it so, one had to remove from it 'the compulsion of economic necessity'.[18] Work remains a duty, but to oneself, for self-fulfillment and to society. Presumably, the removal of economic necessity from work would free people from all undesirable forms of work, widen the range of choices, and benefit both themselves and society at large—Adam Smith's invisible hand in the pursuit of self-interest, but without economic motivation. Remove economic necessity from the motivation to work, and you remove Bentham's pain. Involvement in work becomes a personal choice; which means people can choose work that is more suitable to their desires, more suitable to their natural capacities; work itself becomes all pleasure. This is one of the issues to be addressed in relation to microelectronic technology. If computers, computer-related instruments and telecommunication networks can produce the national output required for a generally rising standard of living, with the participation of a relatively small proportion of the population, the Marxian prophecy may yet be realised, even though the political setting may be somewhat different from that which he envisaged.

Machine Production, Specialisation and Attitudes Towards Work

Today, negative attitudes towards work are commonly associated with routine, monotony, discipline, time-scheduling, and work-process regimentation, not with any physical or mental strain.[19] Charles R. Walker studied changes in a steelmill operation and found a substantial increase in the mental effort required of workers.[20] Telephone operators who changed from manually operated switchboards to automatic ones alleged a considerable increase in mental strain.[21]

But neither the steelmill operation studied by Walker nor the telephone switchboards were truly automatic. What happened in reality was that the operations became semi-automatic, and the operatives, who continued to be required, lost 'control' of some aspects of the operations. The increase in mental strain appears to have been related to increases in the speed of operations, and to the loss of control over the rate of operation. In both cases, it was not automation that increased the mental strain; it was inadequate automation. As the level and scope of automation increases, and less and less critical functions are left at the discretion of the operator, both skill and mental strain will inevitably be somewhat reduced.

It is the specialisation in work, the dictates of machines and processes, and the work routines formulated by others and enforced by others that are the major sources of alienation. Specialisation removed from the worker the product and replaced it with only a part of it, often an infinitesimal part. To paraphrase Neil Chamberlain, a job is no longer a specific undertaking, to be started and completed, with another to follow; it is rather something, a work function, that one does day after day, with little or no variation, as part of a process, but often meaningless by itself.[22] Such a transformation in work activity was dictated by the quest for increase in productivity; specialisation being the instrument of productivity. The combination of specialisation and machine production removed labour from its dominant role in the production process, took away from labour control of the production process, and most important, separated labour from it product.[23]

The response of management to this development has been critical to labour's attitude towards work, and the evolution of production processes. There is no evidence in the literature of any concerted or widespread effort to re-establish worker association and identify with the product, nor is there any evidence of effort to organise production processes in ways which would establish better relationships amongst the workers and between the workers and identifiable segments of the production processes. Some applied the much discussed and now discredited Hawthorne method,[24] and in recent years some experimental successes have been reported from Sweden and Germany. But, most processes remained in the traditional large scale electromechanical infrastructure, with labour performing the complementary functional role dictated by each process. An alternative approach to which management has resorted from time to time is to cause labour to identify with the company. To the extent that the product carried the name of the company – Ford, G.M., G.E. – identification with the company would identify with the product. But, considering the nature of many standardised products, not many workers would have wanted to identify with them. Although some Japanese companies and a few German companies have been successful with such an approach, there is no evidence of widespread worker allegiance to their companies. The ultimate alternative which has gained wide acceptance is to neutralise labour's effect on productivity by making machine operations independent of direct labour participation, or where labour participation continues to be required to make its functional activities passive to the requirements of the production processes. Fully automated systems, such as computer-aided manufacturing and integrated computer–telecommunications systems, are viewed as the ultimate in technological processes which will overcome the remaining human barrier to efficiency. A recent study of work with information technology in two establishments in Great Britain concluded the management's objectives were (1) to reduce human intervention in the production processes; (2) to establish greater control over the processes; and (3) to increase the supervision over operatives.[25]

Throughout the history of industrial development, work specialisation and the placing of mechanical instruments at the disposal of labour were expected to make work not only more efficient, but also easier. That they did: work became more efficient, and considerably less taxing physically; but, for many workers it became mentally dulling. The work performed by workers became progressively more repetitious, undemanding, and monotonous. Perhaps one can tolerate work that is physically and mentally undemanding over short periods of involvement, but the average individual enters the labour market at the age of 18 and remains in it 45 to 50 years! It is difficult to sustain enthusiasm and interest in any work over such a long period, much less for work that does not generate physical or mental stimulus. In this context, it is arguable whether it would not be desirable from a socioeconomic standpoint to eliminate such jobs. But, then another potential socioeconomic problem is created, namely, unemployment. What are the prospects of replacing such undesirable jobs with more satisfying work activities? Recognition that there are monotonous, repetitious, physically demanding or undemanding jobs, and jobs that are mentally numbing, and agreement that such jobs should be changed or eliminated, relates to the demand side of the process only; what about the supply of labour side? Can the people who work at these monotonous, etc. jobs work effectively at jobs that require imagination, initiative and discipline? Is it possible that for a certain proportion of the population the alternative to routine and undemanding jobs is no jobs? What promises are contained in the socio-economic system emerging from microelectronic technology?

All work activities are not, of course, of the nature just described, and the difference suggests perhaps the nature of work that is compatible with human nature. An examination of work activities and processes which people find desirable reveals four general characteristics: *independence* in the carrying out of the work tasks, whether the tasks are indenpendently determined or are required by the nature of the activity, by the nature of the process of production, by rules, regulations or whatever; *variety* in work activities performed day to day and week to week; *flexibility* in the carrying out of the work activities, particularly in starting time, ending time, and time continuity; and free personal *choice* in entering and staying in the work activity. Such characteristics will be found in the work of independent businessmen, farmers, tradesmen, and all kinds of professional people. Warren Bennis is quoted to have said, many such people, particularly professionals 'are committed to the task, not to the job; to their standards, not their boss'.[26] It is instructive to note that such people generally work longer hours than people whose tasks and work routine are presented by employers.[27] But, even in such work activities personal enthusiasm cannot be sustained indefinitely. Most organised work requires commitment on the part of those who undertake to perform it; and for most people the lifetime of commitment to work is too long for sustained enthusiasm, regardless how flexible the work activity itself. Many continue to work for years after retirement, and some work as hard after as before retirement, but often involving work routines in new environments.

Another element in many such work activities that contributes to the satisfaction derived from their performance is the coalescence of work with other activities. There is no separation of work from leisure the way there is in most wage and salary employments. Often it is difficult to determine when work ends. For example, when does a farmer not work? Is a scientist relaxing or working when reading a scientific journal? Is an economist working or relaxing when reading the *Wall Street Journal* or the *Financial Times* at home, at the club, or when commuting to work (hopefully not while driving)? These are important issues in the definition of work, particularly when less and less of work can be packaged into measurable units. A nightmare for bureaucrats and administrators who prefer identification and compartmentalisation of everything, but a relief for people from regimentation. As indicated above, the regimentation, rigidity and discipline imposed on people at work are seldom dictated by the work processes; they are conceived by people, imposed by people, and enforced by people. They are a manifestation of lack of trust in the integrity and responsibility of people in the performance of their work tasks; some are motivated by administrative convenience; some are presumed to be based on efficiency considerations; and some are based on nothing more than established rules whose rationale has long been forgotten.

The emphasis on work for personal fulfillment and psycho-social well-being is a historical reality that is fast fading into the past. Before the advent of product standardisation and mass production, craftsmen and their work associates took pride in what they were doing, and the close relationship between producer and consumer provided opportunities for personal satisfaction. Also, the limited availability of social institutions and recreational opportunities, meant that most social and cultural activities were organised around the place of work. In such an environment, it is natural that work should be a source of fulfillment and a means to social interaction. Separation from work, by retirement or dismissal, meant separation from the reality of daily life.

But, processes of production have changed, and with that the worker–work identification has changed; to most workers, work is nothing more than 'a job that pays.' The majority gain no personal satisfaction from the nature of work they perform; and neither the work itself nor the workplaces where it is performed, are indispensible for psychological and social wellbeing, notwithstanding statements to the contrary, usually made by people who enjoy their work. Some work is enjoyable; and so is work at different periods in ones life time. But, most people are engaged in pretty dull work activities, alongside other people, some of whom are not very pleasant and some quite dull; and when such jobs go on year after year for 30 to 40 years, all excitement and fulfillment has long passed.

Another aspect of work which seems to contribute to worker alienation is the organisation of work processes and ways in which workers are required to participate in them. There is a finality and rigidity in them, as if they are dictated by the technology and forces beyond the control of management. Yet, for the most part they are determined by management. Witness, for example, the variations in work organisation and methods of worker participation amongst production processes using the same technology and performing the same activities. Rigidity in the organisation of work processes and inflexibility in systems of worker participation are frustrating for workers, particularly when they know that alternative forms are superior in relation to both worker satisfaction and productivity. Workers know what technology dictates, and what human decisions dictate; and become alienated when they realise that it is easier to change technology that to change human decisions.

The on-going microelectronic transformation of mechanical and manual processes presents an opportunity for experimentation with alternative forms of work organisations. Indications are that processes can be programmed to be rigid or flexible in relation to human participation. The outcome will depend on management's objectives and attitudes towards workers.[28]

Considering, for example, that interactive communication via computers will make it possible to participate in work activities involving information processing and information communication from any location, at any time, there would be no need for concentration of all workers into offices. A word processor operator with access to the computer and through it to all who have access to it, can be located anywhere. The question is how much physical presence would management deem necessary for effective supervision of work and participation in the work processes. The computer can be made to be an effective supervisor: it can record precisely the time at which it is accessed by anyone; it can record why it was accessed, for how long, at what intervals; it can refuse to accept work after an indicated deadline; it can refuse to give out information after some indicated time; it can be made to be uncompromisingly demanding. Some managers may well attempt to introduce rigidity in work processes and in worker participation, and attribute it to the dictates of the technology. Many have done so; the computer has become the object of much vilification that should properly be directed elsewhere.

A Leisure Society?

Increasing leisure time is a historical reality. Over the years, as economies advanced industrially and commercially, the number of days of work per week, per month and per year decreased, the number of years of work over a lifetime decreased, as people stayed at school longer and retired from work earlier, and the hours of work decreased progressively, from 72 per week, to 60, to 54, 48, 44, 40, to the present range of 32 to 37. In addition, when account is taken of all sorts of leaves from work – some statutory, some contractual, some with special permission, and some discretionary (absenteeism), work-time over the year now averages at no more than about 20 per cent of the total time available to each of us. Advanced industrial-commercial societies have become leisure societies. Work has been increasingly performed by electromechanical slaves. In the US lifetime leisure for men after the age of 14 years has tripled since 1900.[29]

Computers, telecommunications technology and microelectronic instruments give promise that the transfer of work from humans to machines will continue, which will accommodate the indicated desires of the people for still fewer hours of work, more frequent and longer vacations, earlier retirement, and more discretionary time off work without penalty. They give promise also that the transfer of more work from humans to machines will continue to generate increasing quantities of goods and services, and provide increasing living standards.

The critical question about the impact of technology has never been the *transfer of work* from humans to machines, the increase in efficiency, the production of more and different goods and services, and the general increase in living standards. It has been rather, *the taking of work* from humans by machines, and the rendering of humans redundant in relation to work. Since work is the major source of income, and the main avenue to participation in economic, social and political activity, the threat to work is a threat on income and social participation. This is the problem that called for solutions throughout history, and it is the problem that needs to be addressed in relation to microelectronic technology.

Income Security

Economic security is probably more important to the average adult in our society than any other objective. Much of education is taken with a view to increasing economic security; occupational training is generally taken with the same objective in mind; the choice of residence is often influenced by it; the same consideration enters into the choice of employment; choices amongst political parties are influenced by expectations of economic security; and the issue is even considered in the choice of marriage partners. The quest for economic security turns professionals, such as doctors, into agitators for legislative privilege and protection; causes older workers to demand seniority privileges in hiring and firing; makes unions impose make-work rules; and compels politicians to search for alternatives to economic security when employment security cannot be guaranteed.

Until the very recent past economic security was commonly associated with employment security. But, as employment security became increasingly more difficult to sustain, the meaning of economic security has broadened into a combination of employment and income. Governments have taken the position that since employment security cannot be guaranteed in a free enterprise economy, a measure of income security should be provided. Hence the introduction of unemployment insurance payments, welfare payments, income supplements, and such other income support provisions. The arrangements have been generally accepted by the population, but as interim measures only – to provide a reasonable standard of living in periods of interruptions in the continuity of employment. The majority of the working population have not accepted them as possible perfect substitutes for employment.

This failure to accept income security as a substitute for employment security has been interpreted generally to constitute a manifestation that the work ethic is firmly imbedded into the psyche of our society. Whether that is actually the case, or whether it is simply related to the levels of income that are provided outside employment, and to the social organisation of work, leisure and participation in economic and political activity generally, remains to be determined. How would people respond to the choice between income and work if the incomes were equal to what they would earn from work? How would they respond if the organisation of social and political activity were such as to enable them to participate as actively outside the work environment as through it? The progressive decrease in the number of hours and days that people work over the year for increasing incomes, and the increasing demands for more time off work, indicate that although people continue to place priority on secure and continuing employment, they regard it primarily as a source of income and an avenue for social and political participation. They want it secure and continuing, but would rather work fewer hours per day, and days per week; have more time off work; have greater discretion on when to work and when not to work; and earn higher incomes. In this context, the possibility that microelectronic technology will perform increasing amounts of work that people have been performing heretofore, should be a welcome possibility. It will facilitate the quest for less work. Similarly, the possibility that microelectronic technology will increase efficiency in the production of goods and services and thereby increase the national output, should also be a welcome possibility, since it will facilitate the earning of higher incomes.

To the extent that technology will effect employment negatively, it will effect the distribution of employment income. When the population at large participates in the production of the national output, the distribution of the output takes place in accordance with the prices that are paid for the services of the labour, the capital and the land. The respective prices, and the resultant returns are determined by markets, short-term and long-term contracts, governments, institutions, boards, agencies, and all sorts of organised groups. Some of the prices and the related returns reflect the actual contributions made to the output by the recipients, some are excessive relative to the contributions, and some are deficient relative to contributions. It all depends on the market conditions that prevail during the periods when prices are set, and the extent to which individuals, enterprises and organised groups can influence the prices paid to them.[30] Nevertheless, regardless who gets how much, the sum of all payments to the participants will equal the national output.

Those of the population who do not participate in the production of the national output with their labour, their capital or their land, are deemed not to contribute to the output, and therefore, not to have an economic claim on it, even though they may have a social claim. Those amongst them who are dependents of participants share in the share of output received by the participants; while those who are not dependents of participants, and non-participants and their dependents become dependents of government. Governments are deemed to have a social responsibility to take a share from the shares earned by the participating population, and transfer it to non-participants. The determination of how much is taken, from whom, and how much is given, to whom, is largely a political decision, based, of course, on economic reality.

The critical issue in this: as the volume of work activity suitable for human labour continues its historical decline, will the work that remains be spread amongst the people at large as heretofore, or will it be the kind of work that only a relatively small proportion of the population will be able to perform? In the first instance, we will continue on the historical path of less and less work from everyone for more and more income payments; in the second instance, a new social and political order will emerge in which a few will be involved directly in the production of the national output, and governments will take increasing proportions of it to distribute amongst the population at large. In the first instance, employment will remain the primary mechanism for the distribution of the national income; in the second, the mechanism will depend on the social and political organisation of society. It is possible to distribute income amongst non-participants in work activity directly, in the form of social security payments and income supplements; alternatively, a distinction can be made between voluntary non-participants and involuntary non-participants, as at present, and direct payments be given to the former, and work activities be created for the latter. Income distribution through employment creates the impression of equity – to each according to employment position and implied contribution to economy and society. When governments create employment in social and governmental activities, they attain two important goals: create the impression of equitable distribution of income, and increase their powers.

The foregoing suggests that even if videonic telematic systems produce increasing national outputs of goods and services with the assistance of a relatively small proportion of the population, governments will create employment in social, cultural and governmental activities for those who would wish to participate in work activities. Employment will continue to be the main avenue for participation by the population in society, and it will remain the most acceptable mechanism for the distribution of income. The limit to the creation of such employment is (a) the rate of growth in the national output, (b) the share of the output that can be taken from the factors participating in its production without impairing their productive capacities, and (c) society's tolerance of income redistribution.

Notes and References

Chapter 1 Reality and Fiction

1. There is some dispute in the literature on whether workers rioted against the introduction of machines or whether the riots were triggered by hunger and misery. See P. Mantoux, *The Industrial Revolution in the Eighteenth Century* (London: Methuen, 1966) pp. 405–506.
2. Statement at a symposium on 'Modern Technology: Problem or Opportunity?' published in *Daedalus*, (1980). The statements will be found in the discussion on 'Some Issues of Technology', pp. 3–24, and in his paper 'Technology, Evolution, and Purpose', pp. 65–81.
3. J. Hicks, *Capital and Growth* (London: Oxford University Press, 1969) p. 270. By 'gain in technical knowledge' he means application of technical knowledge, not mere invention.
4. W. Z. Hirsh, 'Technological Progress and Microeconomic Theory', *American Economic Review – Papers and Proceedings*, LIX (1969) pp. 36–43. Also P. A. Yotopoulos and J. B. Nugent, *Economics of Development: Empirical Investigations* (New York: Harper & Row, 1976) pp. 145–63.
5. For a good examination of this issue see A. Heertje, *Economics and Technical Change* (London: Werdenfeld & Nicolson, 1977).
6. See, D. Dillard, *Economic Development of the North Atlantic Community*, (Englewood Cliffs, N.J.: Prentice-Hall Inc., 1967) pp. 246–7.
7. N. Wiener, *The Human Use of Human Beings: Cybernetics and Society* (Boston: Houghton Mifflin, 1950) p. 189.
8. A Sorge *et al.*, *Microelectronics in the Workplace: Unity and Diversity of Work Under CNC in Great Britain and West Germany*, paper presented at a EEC conference on Microelectronics (Dublin: 18–20 Nov. 1981).
9. The term 'télématique' was coined by Simon Nora and Alain Minc to indicate the confluence of computers and telecommunications technology. *The Computerization of Society* (Cambridge, Mass.: MIT Press, 1980).
10. D. Dillard, ibid., p. 246.
11. A. Toffler, *The Third Wave* (New York: Bantam Books, 1980).

Chapter 2 Evolution, Revolution and Manpower Adjustments

1. C. R. Fay, *Great Britain from Adam Smith to the Present Day – an Economic and Social Survey* (London: Longmans, Green & Co., 1940) p. 304.
2. UK, Factory Commission, *First Report*, (London: HMSO, 1833) p. 10.
3. C. R. Fay, ibid., p. 353.
4. A. Toffler, ibid., p. 27.
5. For a contrary expression of this see A. Toffler, ibid., pp. 40–1.

6. J. A. Schumpeter, *Capitalism, Socialism and Democracy* (London: Allen & Unwin, 1943) p. 61.
7. ibid., p. 62.
8. ibid., p. 83.
9. For discussion on the subject of internal and external labour markets and adjustments to technological change, see P. B. Doeringer, *Work Force Adjustments in Private Industry – their Implications for Manpower Policy* (Washington, D.C.: Department of Labor, Manpower Administration, Monograph no. 7, Oct. 1968).
10. ibid., p. 102.
11. A good analysis on the actual and potential application of computer technology to industrial activity will be found in a paper by J. Scrimgeour entitled 'CAD/CAM and its Significance to Canadian Industry', presented at the 1975 Annual Congress of EIC, (Winnipeg, Canada: 30 Sept.–3 Oct. 1975).
12. D. Dillard writes: before the organisation of the factory system people were relatively poor, but they had 'a relatively carefree way of life in comparison with which factory employment was viewed as little better than imprisonment', ibid., p. 49.

Chapter 3 The Nature of Microelectronic Technology

1. A. Benjamin, 'This is the Dawning of the "Age of Software"', *Computer Data*, 6 (Apr. 1981) p. 27.
2. A. Heertje, ibid., p. 111.
3. *The Economist*, 283 (8 May 1982) p. 97.
4. H. Brooks, ibid., p. 42.
5. S. Kahne *et al.*, 'Automatic Control by Distributed Intelligence', *Scientific American*, 240 (1979) pp. 78–90.
6. S. Kahne, ibid., pp. 78–90.
7. See paper by J. Scrimgeour, 'An Overview of CAD/CAM in Canada Today' (Ottawa: Department of Industry, Trade and Commerce, Technology Branch, 1980).
8. J. L. Remmerswaal, 'Production Technology in the Metalworking Industry and Employment', in *Proceedings of Workshop on the Relationship Between Technical Development and Employment*, Six Countries Programme on Aspects of Government Policies Towards Technological Innovation in Industry (Paris: 13–14 Nov. 1978).
9. Reference is made on pp. 137–8 to the National Cash Register Company, the Standard Electric Lorenz Company of West Germany, the Ericsson Telecommunications Co. of Sweden, and the Olivetti Company of Italy.
10. G. Bylinsky, 'A New Industrial Revolution is on the Way', *Fortune*, 104 (1981) pp. 106–14.
11. G. Bylinsky quoting D. E. Wisnosky, ibid., p. 110.
12. 282 (30 Jan. 1982) p. 81.
13. Study by Booz, Allen and Hamilton, US Management Consulting firm, quoted in *The Economist*, 282 (30 Jan. 1982) p. 81.

Chapter 4 Stimulants and Barriers

1. For a good survey of the factors responsible for delays in the implementation of electronic systems see: S. Kolodziej, 'Problems Outweigh Advantages . . . So Far', *Computer Data*, 5 (Nov. 1980) pp. 82–6.
2. A brief analysis of the various problems will be found in T. S. Aston, *The Industrial Revolution 1760–1830*, (New York: Oxford University Press, 1961) pp. 56–7.
3. Some of these are detailed in a report by the CAD/CAM Council of Canada, *Interim Report on CAD/CAM Technologies* (Ottawa: July 1979), and other in a paper by J. R. Bessant and K. E. Dickson, *Microelectronics and Manufacturing: The Marriage that Never Was?* presented at a EEC Conference on the Information Society (Dublin: 18–20 Nov. 1981).
4. J. Rada, *The Impact of Micro-Electronics* (Geneva: ILO, 1980) p. 31.
5. J. Scrimgeour, J. R. Dickinson, and D. Bonham, *A Matrix Approach to the Identification of Sectors of the Canadian Economy Most Affected by CAD/CAM Technology* (Ottawa: Department of Industry, Trade and Commerce, Technology Branch, 1979).
6. *The Economist*, 271 (9 June 1979) p. 25.
7. *The Labour Gazette*, 57 (Feb. 1957) pp. 178–9 [Emphasis added].
8. Trade Unions Congress (TUC), *Employment and Technology* (London, 1979).
9. R. Williams and R. Moseley, *The Trade Union Response to Information Technology*, paper presented at a EEC Conference on The Information Society (Dublin: 18–20 Nov. 1981).
10. ibid., p. 15.
11. N. W. Chamberlain, *Remaking American Values* (New York: Basic Books, 1977) pp. 83–9.
12. A. B. Cherns, 'Speculations on the Social Effects of New Microelectronics Technology', *International Labour Review*, 119 (1980) pp. 705–21.

Chapter 5 Development and Application of Technology

1. D. Dillard, ibid., p. 246.
2. D. Dillard, ibid., p. 247.
3. ibid., p. 247.
4. ibid., p. 247.
5. Some of these characteristics are identified by the U.K. Advisory Council for Applied Research and Development (ACARD) in *The Applications of Semiconductor Technology* (London: HMSO, 1978).
6. 'Robots Enter the Industrial Market, *Computer Data*, 5 (Feb. 1980) p. 16.
7. J. K. Galbraith, *The New Industrial State*, (New York: Mentor, 1968) p. 276.
8. D. Brody and D. A. Buchanan, *Information Technology and the Experience of Work*, presented at the EEC Conference on Information Technology and Society (Dublin: 18–20 Nov. 1981).

Chapter 6 Occupations and Occupational Structure

1. For a detailed examination of the subject, see: *Technology and Manpower in the Health Service Industry 1965–1975* (Washington, D.C.: US Department of Labor, Bulletin no. 14, 1967).
2. M. U. Porat found that 46 per cent of the Gross National Product of the U.S. was 'bound-up' with information activity, and nearly half of the labour force of the US was engaged in some sort of 'informational' activity. *The Information Economy: Definition and Measurement* (Washington, D.C.: US Department of Commerce, May 1977) p. 1.
3. J. K. Galbraith, ibid., p. 74.
4. The end of the Second World War in 1945 did not end the war economy. Peace was followed by the cold war and continued rearmament, to which then the Korean war was superimposed in the 1950s.
5. A. J. Schumpeter, *The Theory of Economic Development* (Cambridge, Mass: Harvard University Press, 1934).
6. Daniel Bell makes such a statement in *The Coming of Post-Industrial Society* (New York: Basic Books 1973) pp. 126–7.
7. I. Barron and R. Curnow, *The Future with Microelectronics: Forecasting the Effects of Information Technology* (London: Frances Pinter, 1979) pp. 189–90.
8. This trend is well established. Institutions should demonstrate their resolve to arrest its spread and eventually reverse it. See H. R. Bowen, *The State of the Nation and the Agenda for Higher Education*, (San Francisco: Jossey-Bass Inc., 1982).
9. See detailed discussion on this subject in *Work Force Adjustments in Private Industry – Their Implications for Manpower Policy*, (Washington, D.C.: US Department of Labor, 1968) pp. 104–6.
10. Mention should be made of the fact that such transfers result in an increase in the average level of the work-functions performed by each of the occupations involved. When increases in wages and salaries accompany such adjustments, they are as much related to the increase in average value of the work-functions performed, as they are to the forces of demand and supply.
11. F. O. Setzer, *Technological Change Over the Life of a Product: Changes in Skill Inputs and Production Processes* (unpublished Ph.D. Dissertation, Yale University, 1974).
12. See the author's report on *The Effect of Technological Changes on Educational and Skill Requirements of Industry* (Ottawa: Department of Industry, Trade and Commerce, 1978) pp. 119–54.

Chapter 7 Effects on Occupations and Skills

1. M. U. Porat, ibid., pp. 104–35.
2. For US projections through 1990, see: M. L. Carey, 'Occupational Employment Growth Through 1990', *Monthly Labor Review* 104 (Aug. 1981) pp. 42–55.
3. The rate for all occupations to 1990 is projected at about 22 per cent.

4. M. L. Carey, ibid., p. 46.
5. J. R. Bright, 'The Relationship of Increasing Automation and Skill Requirements', in *Report of the U.S. National Commission on Technology, Automation and Economic Progress*, Appendix, vol. II (Washington, D.C.: U.S. Government Printing Office, 1966) p. 208.
6. A significant relationship between education and the capacity to adjust successfully to changes in machinery was found by a number of investigators. See E. Mueller et al., *Technological Advance in an Expanding Economy* (Ann Arbor: University of Michigan, Institute for Social Research, 1969).
7. J. R. Bright, ibid., p. 208.
8. Ibid., p. 208.
9. A. J. Jaffe and J. Froomkin, *Technology and Jobs* (New York: Praeger, 1968) p. 91.
10. S. G. Peitchinis, *The Effect of Technological Changes on Educational and Skill Requirements of Industry* (Research Report, 1978) pp. 155–62.
11. F. Lynn, 'An Investigation of the Rate of Development and Diffusion of Technology in Our Modern Industrial Society', *Report of the U.S. National Commission on Technology, Automation and Economic Progress*, appendix, vol. II, (Washington, D.C.: 1966) pp. 11–39.
12. Ibid., pp. 87–9.
13. Ibid., p. 89.
14. J. R. Bright, *Automation and Management* (Cambridge, Mass: Harvard Business School, 1958) ch. 12.
15. S. A. Fine, *The Nature of Automated Jobs and Their Educational and Training Requirements* (McLean, Va.: Human Sciences Research Inc., 1964).
16. S. G. Peitchinis, ibid.
17. See E. Mueller *et al.*, ibid.
18. His references to education and skills relate to skill requirements as a result of switching to new techniques; there is no discussion on the relationship between prevailing levels of education and skills and the introduction of new techniques. See E. Mansfield, *The Economics of Technological Change* (New York: W. W. Norton, 1968) pp. 138–42.
19. S. Mobert, Under Secretary of the Swedish Ministry of Education makes reference to this Issue in 'Technological Change and its Implications for Education', *Proceedings of an International Conference on Automation, Full Employment and a Balanced Economy* (Washington, D.C.: The American Foundation on Automation and Employment Inc., 1967).

Chapter 8 Employment Effects: Establishment and Economy

1. It is instructive to note that it is not necessary to assume an actual decrease in employment to create excessive unemployment. All one need assume is lack of increase in employment or increase in employment by less than the increase in the labour force.
2. This is the sort of reasoning to be found in C. Jenkins and B. Sherman, *The Collapse of Work* (London: Eyre Methuen, 1979) and H. Menzies, *Women and the Chip* (Montreal: The Institute for Research on Public Policy, 1981).

3. *Microelectronics at Work: Productivity and Jobs in the World Economy* (Washington, D.C.: Worldwatch Institute, Paper 39, Oct. 1980) p. 29.
4. C. Jenkins and B. Sherman, *The Collapse of Work* (London: Eyre Methuen 1979); I. Barron and R. C. Curnow, ibid.; C. Freeman, 'Technical Change and Future Employment Prospects in Industrialised Societies', in *Proceedings of Workshop on the Relationship Between Technical Development and Employment*, Six Countries Programme on Aspects of Government Policies Towards Technological Innovation in Industry (Paris: 13–14 Nov. 1978); and T. Stonier, *Technological Change and the Future*, paper presented at the 1979 Annual Meeting of the British Association for the Advancement of Science.
5. European Trade Union Institute, *The Impact of Microelectronics on Employment in Western Europe in the 1980s* (Brussels: 1970).
6. I. Barron and R. C. Curnow, ibid.
7. ETUI., ibid.
8. ETUI., ibid.
9. G. Friedrichs, *Microelectronics – a New Dimension of Technological Change and Automation* (paper presented at a Club of Rome Conference in West Berlin, 3–6 Oct. 1979) p. 7.
10. J. Rada, ibid., p. 351.
11. G. Friedrichs, ibid., pp. 9–10.
12. C. Hines and G. Searle, *Automatic Unemployment* (London: Earth Resources Research, 1979). Gains in productivity in excess of 100 per cent were also reported by the U.K. Central Policy Review Staff in *Social and Employment Implications of Microelectronics* (London: mimeo, 1978) pp. 7–8.
13. S. Nora and A. Minc, ibid., pp. 7–8.
14. Reported in *New Technology* (Detroit, Mich.: United Automobile Workers, Summer 1978).
15. B. Lamborghini, *The Diffusion of Microelectronics in Industrial Companies* (The Olivetti Company, Torino, Italy, mimeo, 1980).
16. S. G. Peitchinis, *The Employment Implications of Computers and Telecommunications Technology* (Ottawa: Department of Communications 1981).
17. *The Economist*, 278 (3 Jan. 1981).
18. C. Freeman, ibid., p. 8.
19. In 1950 it was 37.5 per cent of the civilian labour force; in 1960, 33 per cent; in 1970, 28.4 per cent; in 1980, 23.1 per cent.
20. T. Stonier, ibid., p. 6.
21. If employment in goods-producing and services-producing processes in the US were to stabilise at the current levels, and the projected labour force of about 125 million in 1990 were to materialise, unemployment in 1990 will be around 24 per cent.
22. The proposition that some jobs may not be functionally related to production processes and that their creation and continuing existence depends on growth is not new. Mercantilists (16th and 17th centuries) and Physiocrats (17th and 18th centuries) discussed the issue in the context of 'productive' and 'unproductive' labour. O. H. Taylor, *A History of Economic Thought* (New York: McGraw-Hill Book Company, 1960).

23. D. W. Morse and S. H. Gray, *Early Retirement – Boon or Bane? a Survey of Three Large Corporations* (Montclair, N.Y.: Allanheld, Osmun & Co., 1980).

Chapter 9 Work and Leisure

1. Scholarly writings abound on the work ethic, work motivation, work and leisure, but not on the concept of work. It is generally taken for granted that the concept is well defined; but it is not. See M. Mead, *The Changing Cultural Patterns of Work and Leisure* (Washington D.C.: US Department of Labor, 1967); D. Bell, *The Coming of Post Industrial Society* (New York: Bantam Books, 1973); P. C. Smith *et al.*, *The Measurement of Satisfaction in Work and Retirement* (Chicago: Rand McNally & Co., 1969); H. Borow, *Man in a World at Work* (Boston: Houghton Mifflin, 1964); S. Nosow and W. H. Form (eds), *Man, Work and Society* (New York: Basic Books, 1962); M. D. Dunnett (ed.), *Work and Non-Work in the Year 2001* (Monterey, Calif.: Brooks/Cole Publishing Company, 1973).
2. To the extent that the amateur is a learner, it is deemed that the activities are learning activities, and as such they are an investment which will yield returns in future. But, is the work of a student not work because it is investment?
3. See: Karl Marx, *Theories of Surplus-Value* (vol. IV of *Capital*), part I (Moscow: Progress Publishers, Burns trans. 1969).
4. M. Mead, ibid., p. 10.
5. Time-budget data of average wage-salary earner in the US. J. P. Robinson, *Social Change as Measured by Time-Budgets*, paper presented at the 1966 Annual Meeting of the American Sociological Association, Cited in T. Scitovsky, *The Joyless Economy* (New York: Oxford University Press, 1976) p. 163.
6. A. Toffler, ibid.; S. Nora and A. Minc, ibid., I. Barron and R. C. Curnow, ibid.
7. J. Gershuny, *After Industrial Society? The Emerging Self-Service Economy* (London: Macmillan, 1978).
8. Aristotle, *The Nichomachean Ethics*, Racklam trans., book X, ch. 7.
9. Aristotle, ibid., book X, ch. 6.
10. J. D. Owen, *The Price of Leisure* (Montreal: McGill-Queen's University Press, 1969) p. 5.
11. S. Kuznets, *Economic Change* (New York: W. W. Norton, 1953) p. 208.
12. M. Mead, ibid., p. 15.
13. A. Gray, *The Development of Economic Doctrine* (London: Longmans, Green & Co., 1951) p. 14.
14. Cicero, *De Officiis*, book I, xlii, Loeb trans., pp. 153–5.
15. Aristotle makes reference to 'natural' capacities in his discourse on slavery. He distinguishes between 'natural slaves' and those who 'contrary to the intention of Nature . . . possess the bodies (but) not the souls of free men . . .', *Politics*, books I, ch. 6, Welldon trans., p. 13.
16. A. Gray, ibid., p. 45.
17. E. Fromm, *Marx's Concept of Man* (New York: Unger, 1961).

18. T. Scitovsky, ibid., p. 90.
19. Scitovsky provides a fairly comprehensive list of studies on the issue, carried out largely by psychologists and sociologists, ibid., pp. 89–105, 206–8, 279–89.
20. *Toward an Automated Factory* (Princeton, N.J.: Yale University Press, 1957).
21. Studies by the author.
22. N. W. Chamberlain, *Remaking American Values* (New York: Basic Books, 1977) p. 84.
23. Scitovsky comments that only artists, writers, professional people and a few craft occupations still get satisfaction out of their work. 'The majority of mankind has been alienated from its produce.' ibid., p. 207.
24. The Hawthorne experiments involved changes in working conditions to increase productivity. They were carried out at Western Electric's Hawthorne plant near Chicago, from 1924 to 1932. Recent investigations of the Research methods used and the conclusions reached on the basis of the evidence cast serious doubt on the validity of the reported results. See Berkeley Rice, 'The Hawthorne Defect: Persistence of a Flawed Theory', *Psychology Today* (Feb. 1982) pp. 70–4.
25. D. Brody and D. A. Buchanan, *Information Technology and the Experience of Work*, paper presented at the EEC Conference on Information Technology (Dublin: 18–20 Nov. 1981).
26. Quoted by Toffler, *Future Shock* (New York: Random House, 1970) p. 148.
27. Scitovsky, ibid., p. 93.
28. A good paper on the issue is D. Brody and D. A. Buchanan, ibid.
29. S. A. Levitan and C. M. Johnson, *Second Thoughts on Work* (Kalamazoo, Mich.: W. E. Upjohn Institute, 1982) p. 48.
30. L. C. Thurow, *Generating Ineuqlity: Mechanisms of Distribution in the U.S. Economy* (New York: Basic Books, 1975).

Selected Bibliography

Aristotle, *The Nichomachean Ethics*, book x, Racklam trans.

Arthur D. Little Inc., *Strategic Impact of Intelligence Electronics in U.S. and Western Europe: 1977–1987* (London: ADL, 1979).

Association of Professional, Executive, Clerical and Computer Staff, *Office Technology: The Trade Union Response* (London: 1979).

Association of Scientific, Technical and Managerial Staffs, *Technological Change and Collective Bargaining* (London: ASTMS, 1979).

Aston, T. S., *The Industrial Revolution 1760–1830* (New York: Oxford University Press, 1961).

Barron, I. and Curnow, R., *The Future with Microelectronics: Forecasting the Effects of Information Technology* (London: Frances Pinter, 1979).

Bell, D., *The Coming of Post-Industrial Society* (New York: Basic Books 1973).

Best, F. (ed.), *The Future of Work*, (Englewood Cliffs N.J.: Prentice-Hall, 1973).

Bhalla, A. S. (ed.), *Technology and Employment in Industry* (Geneva: ILO, 1975).

Borow, H., *Man in a World at Work* (Boston: Houghton Mifflin, 1964).

Bowen, H. R., *The State of the Nation and the Agenda for Higher Education*, (San Francisco: Jossey-Bass Inc., 1982).

Bright, J. R., *Automation and Management* (Cambridge, Mass: Harvard Business School, 1958).

Bright, J. R., 'The Relationship of Increasing Automation and Skill Requirements,' in *Report of the U.S. National Commission on Technology, Automation and Economic Progress*, appendix, vol. II (Washington D.C.: Government Printing Office, 1966).

British Association for the Advancement of Science (The), *Technology and the Future of Work* (London: 1978).

Chamberlain, N. W., *Remaking American Values* (New York: Basic Books 1977).

Coombs, R., and Green, K., *The Effect of Microelectronic Technologies On Employment Prospects* (London: Gower Publishing Co., 1980).

Dertouzos, M. L., and Moses, J., (eds), *The Computer Age: A Twenty-Year View* (Cambridge, Mass: MIT Press, 1980).

Dillard, D., *Economic Development of the North Atlantic Community*, (Englewood Cliffs, N.J.: Prentice-Hall, 1967).

Doeringer, P. B. and Piore, M. J., *Internal Labor Markets, Technological Change and Labor Force Adjustments* (Cambridge, Mass: Harvard University Press, 1966).

Dunnette, M. D., (ed.), *Work and Nonwork in the Year 2001* (Monterey, Calif.: Brooks/Cole, 1973).

Evans, J., *The Impact of Microelectronics on Employment in Western Europe in the 1980s* (Brussels: European Trade Union Institute, 1979).

Fechter, A., *Forecasting the Impact of Technological Change on Manpower Utilization and Displacement: an Analytic Summary* (Washington, D.C.: Urban Institute, 1975).

Fine, S. A., *The Nature of Automated Jobs and their Educational and Training Requirements*, (McLean Va.: Human Sciences Research Inc. 1964).

Forester, T., (ed.), *The Microelectronics Revolution: The Complete Guide to the New Technology and Its Impact on Society* (Cambridge, Mass: MIT Press, 1981).

Freeman, C., 'Technical Change and Future Employment Prospects in Industrialised Societies', in *Proceedings of Workshop on the Relationship between Technical Development and Employment*, Six Countries Programme on Aspects of Government Policy Towards Technological innovation in Industry (Paris: 13–14 Nov. 1978).

Freeman, C., Clark, J., and Soete, L., *Unemployment and Technical Innovation: A Study of Long Waves and Economic Development* (London: Frances Pinter, 1982).

Friedricks, G. and Schaff, A., (eds), *Microelectronics and Society: for Better or for Worse; a Report to the Club of Rome* (Oxford: Pergamon Press, 1982).

Fromm, E., *Marx's Concept of Man* (New York: Unger, 1961).

Froomkin, J., and Jaffe, A. J., *Technology and Jobs: Automation in Perspective* (New York: Praeger, 1968).

Fuchs, V., *The Service Economy* (New York: Columbia University Press, 1968).

Galbraith, J. K., *The Affluent Society* (London: Hamish Hamilton, 1958).

Galbraith, J. K., *The New Industrial State* (Boston: Houghton Mifflin, 1967).

Gendron, B., *Technology and the Human Condition* (New York: St. Martin's Press, 1977).

Gershuny, J., *After Industrial Society: The Emerging Self-Service Economy* (London: Macmillan, 1978).

Gilder, G., *Wealth and Poverty* (New York: Bantam Books, 1981).

Glasser, R., *Leisure: Penalty or Prize?* (London: Macmillan, 1970).

Gotlieb, C. C., and Borodin, A., *Social Issues in Computing*, (New York: Academic Press, 1973).

Great Britain, Central Policy Review Staff, *Social and Employment Implications of Microelectronics* (London: HMSO, 1978).

Heertje, A., *Economics and Technical Change* (London: Werdenfeld & Nicholson, 1977).

Hicks, J., *Capital and Growth* (London: Oxford University Press, 1969).

Hiestand, D. L., *High Level Manpower and Technological Change in the Steel Industry: Implications for Corporate Manpower Planning* (New York: Praeger, 1974).

Hines, C., *The Chips Are Down: The Future Impact of Microprocessors and Computers on Employment in Britain* (London: Earth Resources Research, 1978).

Hines, C., and Searle, G., *Automatic Unemployment* (London: Earth Resources Research, 1979).

Inglehart, R., *The Silent Revolution: Changing Values and Political Styles Among Western Publics* (Princeton, N. J.: Princeton University Press, 1977).

International Data Corporation, 'Information Systems for Tomorrow's Office', a report in the form of an advertisement, in *Fortune*, 106 (18 October 1982) various pages, from p. 17 to p. 82.

International Labour Office, *Effects of Technological Changes on Conditions of Work and Employment in Postal and Telecommunications Services* (Geneva: ILO, 1977).

Japan Computer Usage Development Institute (JACUDI), *Social and Economic Effects of Information Oriented Investment* (Tokyo: 1974).

Japan, Ministry of International Trade and Industry, *A Fact Finding Study on the Impacts of Microelectronics on Employment* (Tokyo: 1979).

Jequier, N. (ed.), *Appropriate Technology: Problems and Promises* (Paris: OECD, Development Centre, 1976).

Jenkins, C. and Sherman, B., *The Collapse of Work* (London: Eyre Methuen, 1979).

Jones, T., (ed.), *Microelectronics and Society* (London: The Open University Press, 1980).

Kahn-Freund, Otto, *Labour Relations: Heritage and Adjustements* (Oxford: Oxford University Press, 1979).

Kamrany, N. M., and Day, R. H., (eds), *Economic Issues of the Eighties*, (Baltimore: The Johns Hopkins University Press, 1979).

Kendall, P. M. H. *et al., The Impact of Chip Technology on Employment and the Labour Market* (London: Metra Consulting Group Ltd., 1980).

Kerr, C. and Rosow, J. M., (eds), *Work in America: The Decade Ahead* (New York: Van Norstrand Reinhold, 1979).

Keynes, J. M., *The General Theory of Employment, Interest and Money* (London: Macmillan, 1961).

Krishnan, K., *Prophecy and Progress: The Sociology of Industrial and Post-Industrial Society* (Harmondsworth: Penguin Books, 1978).

Kuznets, S., *Economic Change* (New York: W. W. Norton, 1953).

Lamberton, D., *Social Costs of Change, Employment, Professional Skills and Curricula* (Paris: OECD, 1978).

Levitan, S., and Johnson, C. M., *Second Thoughts on Work* (Kalamazoo, Mich.: The UpJohn Institute, 1982).

Levien, R. E., *The Emerging Technology: Instructional Uses of the Computer in Higher Education* (New York: The Carnegie Commission on Higher Education and the Rand Corporation, 1972).

Lund, R. T., et al., *Industrialization Automation – Its Nature, Effects and Management: Critical Issues Report* (Cambridge, Mass.: MIT Centre for Policy Alternatives, 1978).

Lund, R. T., *et al., Microprocessor Applications: Cases and Observations*, Report for the Office of the Chief Scientist, Department of Industry of the UK (Cambridge, Mass.: MIT Centre for Policy Alternatives, 1979).

Lynn, F., 'An Investigation of the Rate of Development and Diffusion of Technology in Our Modern Industrial Society', in *Report of the U.S. National Commission on Technology, Automation and Economic Progress*, Appendix, vol. II (Washington, D.C.: Government Printing Office, 1966).

Magnum, G. L., *Adjustment to Technological Change* (Washington, D.C.: Office of National Research and Development Assessment, 1973).

Mansfield, E., *Industrial Research and Technological Innovation: an Econometric Analysis* (New York: W. W. Norton, 1968).

Mansfield, E., *The Economics of Technological Change* (New York: W. W. Norton, 1968).
Mansfield, E., *et al.*, *The Production and Application of New Industrial Technology* (New York: W. W. Norton, 1977).
Mantoux, P., *The Industrial Revolution in the Eighteenth Century* (London: Methuen, 1966).
Martin, J., *Telematic Society: A Challenge for Tomorrow* (Englewood Cliffs, N.J.: Prentice-Hall, 1981).
Masuda, Y., *Social and Economic Effects of Information-Oriented Investment* (Tokyo: Jacudi, 1974).
McClelland, D. C., *The Achieving Society* (New York: Van Norstrand, 1961).
Menzies, H., *Women and the Chip* (Montreal: Institute for Research on Public Policy, 1981).
Mesthene, E. G., *Technological Change: Its Impact on Man and Society* (Cambridge, Mass.: Harvard University Press, 1970).
Minc, A., and Nora, S., *The Computerization of Society* (Boston: MIT Press, 1980).
Morse, D. W., and Gray, S. H., *Early Retirement – Boon or Bane? a Survey of Three Large Corporations* (Montclair, N.Y.: Allanheld, Osman & Co., 1980).
Norman, C., *Microelectronics at Work: Productivity and Jobs in the World Economy* (Washington, D.C.: Worldwatch Institute Paper no. 39, 1980).
Nosow, S., and Form, W. H., (eds), *Man, Work and Society* (New York: Basic Books, 1969).
OECD, *Information Activities, Electronics and Telecommunications Technologies*, vol. I: Impact on Employment, Growth and Trade (Paris: 1981).
OECD, *Technical Change and Economic Policy: Science and Technology in New Economic Context* (Paris: 1980).
Okun, A., *Equality and Efficiency: the Big Trade-off* (Washington, D.C.: The Brookings Institution, 1975).
Owen, J. D., *The Price of Leisure* (Montreal: McGill-Queen's University Press, 1969).
Porat, M. U., *The Information Economy* (Palo Alto, Calif.: Stanford University, Centre for Interdisciplinary Research, 1976).
——, *The Information Economy: Definition and Measurement* (Washington, D.C.: U.S. Department of Commerce, Office of Telecommunications, 1977).
——, *The Information Economy: Sources and Methods for Measuring the Primary Information Sector (Detailed Industry Reports)* (Washington, D.C.: U.S. Department of Commerce, Office of Telecommunications, 1977).
Rabeau, Y., *Tele-informatics, Productivity and Employment: an Economic Interpretation* (Montreal: GAMMA Group, 1980).
Rada, J., *The Impact of Microelectronics* (Geneva: ILO, 1980).
Remmerswaal, J. L., 'Production Technology in the Metalworking Industry and Employment', in *Proceedings of Workshop on the Relationship Between Technical Development and Employment*, Six Countries Programme on Aspects of Government Policies Towards Technological Innovation in Industry (Paris: 13–14 Nov. 1978).
Rosow, J. M., (ed.), *The Worker and the Job: Coping with Change* (Englewood Cliffs, N.J.: Prentice-Hall, 1974).
Rothwell, R., and Zegveld, W., *Technical Change and Employment* (New York: St. Martin's Press, 1980).

Schnailberg, A., *The Environment: From Surplus to Scarcity* (New York: Oxford University Press, 1980).
Schumacher, E. F., *Small is Beautiful: Economics as if People Mattered* (New York: Harper and Row, 1973).
Schumpeter, J. A., *Capitalism, Socialism, and Democracy* (London: Allen & Unwin, 1943).
Schumpeter, J. A., *The Theory of Economic Development* (Cambridge, Mass: Harvard University Press, 1934).
Science Council of Canada, *Planning Now for an Information Society: Tomorrow is Too Late* (Ottawa: Information Canada, 1982).
Science Policy Research Unit, *Microelectronics and Women's Employment In Britain* (Brighton: Sussex University, SPRU Occasional Paper Series, no. 17, 1982).
Scitovsky, T., *The Joyless Economy* (New York: Oxford University Press, 1976).
Setzer, F. O., *Technological Change over the Life of a Product: Changes in Skill Inputs and Production Processes* (Ph.D. Thesis, Yale University, 1974).
Sheehan, B. S., (ed.), *Information Technology: Innovations and Applications* (San Francisco: Jossey-Bass Inc., 1982).
Sherman, B., *et al.*, *Technological Change, Employment and the Need For Collective Bargaining* (London: ASTM, 1979).
Siemens, A. G. (Company), *Buero 1990*, unpublished Report (Munich: 1976).
Sleigh, J., *et al.*, *The Manpower Implications of Micro-electronic Technology* (London: HMSO, 1979).
Somers, G. H., *et al.*, *Adjusting to Technological Change*, Industrial Relations Research Association Series (New York: Harper & Row, 1963).
Stebbins, R. A., *Amateurs: On the Margin Between Work and Leisure* (Beverly Hills, Calif.: Gage, 1979).
Steiber, J., (ed.), *Employment Problems of Automation and Advanced Technology: an International Perspective* (New York: St. Martin's Press, 1966).
Stoneman, P., 'The Effects of Computers on the Demand for Labour in the United Kingdom', *The Economic Journal*, 85 (Sept. 1975) pp. 590–606.
Strassman, P. A., 'The Office of the Future: Information Management for the New Age', *Technology Review*, 82 (Dec. 79/Jan. 80) pp. 54–65.
Traviss, I., *The Computer Impact* (Englewood Cliffs, N.J.: Prentice-Hall, 1970).
Traviss, I., and Gerber, W., *Technology and Work* (Cambridge, Mass.: Harvard University, Program on Technology and Society, Research Review no. 2, 1969).
Thompson, G. B., *Memo from Mercury: Information Technology is Different* (Montreal: Institute for Research on Public Policy, 1979).
Thurow, L. C., *Generating Inequality: Mechanisms of Distribution in the U.S. Economy* (New York: Basic Books, 1975).
Thurow, L. C., *The Zero-Sum Society: Distribution and the Possibilities for Economic Change* (New York: Basic Books, 1980).
Toffler, A., *Future Shock* (New York: Random House, 1970).
Toffler, A., *The Third Wave* (New York: Bantam Books, 1980).
Trade Union Congress (TUC), *Employment and Technology* (London, 1979).
UK Advisory Council for Applied Research and Development (ACARD), *The Applications of Semiconductor Technology* (London: HMSO, 1978).

UK, Central Policy Review Staff, *Social and Employment Implications of Microelectronics*, (London: 1978).

US Bureau of Labour Statistics, *Adjustments to the Introduction of Office Automation*, Bulletin no. 1276 (Washington, D.C.: U.S. Government Printing Office, 1960).

US Congress, House Committee on Science and Technology, *Survey of Science and Technology Issues Present and Future*, Staff Report, 97th Congress, 1st Session (Washington, D.C.: 1981).

US Congress, Office of Technology Assessment, *An Assessment of National Information Systems and Their Effects on Society* (Washington, D.C.: 1979).

US Department of Commerce, *The Role of New Technical Enterprises in the U.S. Economy*, Report of the Commerce Advisory Board to the Secretary of Commerce (Washington, D.C.: Jan. 1976).

US Department of Labor, Office of Manpower Policy, *Manpower Implications of Automation* (Washington, D.C.: 1965).

US Department of Labor, *Technology and Manpower in the Health Service Industry, 1965–1975* (Washington, D.C.: 1967).

US Department of Labor, *Work Force Adjustments in Private Industry – their Implications for Manpower Policy* (Washington, D.C.: 1968).

United States, National Commission on Technology, Automation and Economic Progress, *The Outlook for Technological Change and Employment* (Washington, D.C.: US Government Printing Office, 1966).

United States, National Commission on Technology, Automation and Economic Progress, *Technology and the American Economy*, vol. I (Washington, D.C.: 1966).

——, *The Outlook for Technological Change and the American Economy*, appendix vol. I (Washington, D.C.: 1966).

——, *The Employment Impact of Technological Change*, appendix, vol. II (Washington, D.C.: 1966).

——, *Adjusting to Change*, appendix, vol. III (Washington, D.C.: 1966).

——, *Educational Implications of Technological Change*, appendix, vol. IV (Washington, D.C.: 1966).

Valaskakis, K., *The Information Society: the Issue and the Choices* (Montreal: GAMMA Information Society, 1979).

Walker, C. A., *Toward an Automated Factory* (Princeton, N.J.: Yale University Press, 1957).

Wiener, N., *The Human Use of Human Beings: Cybernetics and Society* (Boston: Houghton Mifflin, 1950).

Zeman, Z. P., *The Impacts of Computer/Communications on Employment: an Overview of Current OECD Debates* (Montreal: Institute for Research on Public Policy, 1979).

Index